Contents at a Glance

Table of Contents

About the Author

Steven Holzner is the award-winning author of more than 100 books, specializing in online topics like Google Buzz. He's been a contributing editor of *PC Magazine* and has specialized in online computing for many years. His books have sold more than 2.5 million copies and have been translated into 18 languages. Steve graduated from MIT and earned his PhD at Cornell. He's been a very popular member of the faculty at both MIT and Cornell, teaching thousands of students over the years. He also runs his own software company and teaches weeklong classes to corporate programmers around the country.

Dedication

To Nancy, of course.

We Want to Hear from You!

As the reader of this book, *you* are our most important critic and commentator. We value your opinion and want to know what we're doing right, what we could do better, what areas you'd like to see us publish in, and any other words of wisdom you're willing to pass our way.

You can email or write me directly to let me know what you did or didn't like about this book—as well as what we can do to make our books stronger.

Please note that I cannot help you with technical problems related to the topic of this book, and that due to the high volume of mail I receive, I might not be able to reply to every message.

When you write, please be sure to include this book's title and author as well as your name and phone or email address. I will carefully review your comments and share them with the author and editors who worked on the book.

E-mail: consumer@samspublishing.com

Mail: Greg Wiegand
          Associate Publisher
          Sams Publishing
          800 East 96th Street
          Indianapolis, IN 46240 USA

Reader Services

Visit our website and register this book at informit.com/register for convenient access to any updates, downloads, or errata that might be available for this book.

Introduction

Welcome to Gmail! This book is all about Google's fantastically popular online mail program, in use by tens of millions of people.

Gmail is the most popular online mail application in the world. You'll see the reasons for that in this book as you get the full Gmail story. You may be new to Gmail, or you may have used it for years—either way there's a lot coming up in this book for you.

Gmail originally started off as a simple mail program, but it has become more elaborate and powerful. Now you can choose your own level—from basic to super-advanced, Gmail has room for everyone. Whereas the early Gmail was very basic to use, today it can take a little more work to become a Gmail-meister, and the goal of this book is to make that process as effortless as possible.

Want to become a Gmail-meister? Stay tuned, you've come to the right book.

What's in This Book

You're going to get a complete tour of Gmail in this book. That means the Gmail story. You'll see what makes Gmail tick and how to make it easy.

Gmail gives you more than any other online mail program, and a lot more than nearly all desktop mail programs. All the features you'd expect are here—easy composing of mail messages, easy sending, formatting, and reading, and so on. But more than that, Gmail is packed with cool features too numerous to name here—although a starter list can't hurt:

▶ Vacation responder to let people know you're on vacation when they send you mail.

▶ The best spam filter in the world. Many people come to Gmail for that reason alone—to never see spam again.

▶ Automatic forwarding of your mail, which can be useful if you just want to run your mail through Gmail to kill spam.

- ▶ Spell-checking for your mail.

- ▶ An address book that automatically adds people (called *contacts* in Gmail).

- ▶ Autocompletion of email addresses as you type them.

- ▶ 7.5GB of space to archive your mail (never delete another mail message!).

- ▶ The most advanced mail search capabilities available (search by date range, who the mail messages were from or to, whether the messages have attachments, search only sent mail, and so on).

- ▶ Easy ways to organize your mail with a few clicks.

And it's still all free.

That's all not even counting Buzz, Gmail's built-in mini-messaging system (like Google's version of Twitter). Buzz comes with Gmail, meaning when you sign up for Gmail, you also get Buzz.

With Buzz, you post short messages for others to see and they can post messages for you to see. You "follow" people to indicate to Buzz that you want to read their posts, and other people follow you. The complete Buzz story is coming up in Lessons 7 and 8.

In addition to all this, there's Google Chat, which is also part of Gmail. Gmail lets you send mail to other people; Buzz lets you see what you post; and Chat speeds it all up by letting you type back and forth interactively with others.

You can chat with a single person or with multiple people at the same time. Everything they type, you can see; everything you type, they can see. You can even search a transcript of your chat sessions in Gmail. In fact, now audio and video chats are available as well.

All in all, there's a lot coming up on your guided tour!

Conventions Used in This Book

Whenever you need to click a particular button or link in Buzz or one of the other sites described in this book, you'll find the label or name for that item in bold type in the text, such as "click the **Create an Account** button." In addition to the text and figures in this book, you'll also encounter some special boxes labelled Tip, Note, or Caution.

> TIP: Tips offer helpful shortcuts or easier ways to do something.

> NOTE: Notes are extra bits of information related to the text that might help you expand your knowledge or understanding.

> CAUTION: Cautions are warnings or other important information you need to know about the consequences of using a feature or executing a task.

Screen Captures

The figures captured for this book are mainly from the Mozilla Firefox web browser. If you use a different browser, your screens might look slightly different.

Also, keep in mind that the Google developers are constantly working to improve their websites and the services offered on them. New features are added regularly to Gmail, and other web services and old ones change or disappear. This means Gmail changes often, so your own screens might differ from the ones shown in this book. Don't be too alarmed, however. The basics, though they are tweaked in appearance from time to time, stay mostly the same in principle and usage.

What You'll Need

You won't need much to work with Gmail—really just an Internet connection and a browser that Google approves of. Here's the list of fully accepted browsers:

- ▶ Google Chrome
- ▶ Firefox 2.0+
- ▶ Internet Explorer 6.0+ (Internet Explorer 7.0+ recommended)
- ▶ Safari 3.0+

These browsers will also work but won't support the latest features:

- ▶ IE 5.5+
- ▶ Netscape 7.1+
- ▶ Mozilla 1.4+
- ▶ Firefox 0.8+
- ▶ Safari 1.3+

If your browser is not listed above, you'll be directed to a page that uses only basic HTML for Gmail. Here are the browsers that will cause that page to display

- ▶ IE 4.0+
- ▶ Netscape 4.07+
- ▶ Opera 6.03+

Your browser needs to have JavaScript and cookies both turned on to use Gmail, and that's all you need.

Ready to get started? Turn to Lesson 1.

LESSON 1

Essential Gmail

Welcome to Gmail, Google's famous online mail program used by millions of people. In this lesson, you'll get a guided tour of what Gmail can do.

Gmail is the world's most popular online mail program, and you're going to see just why that is in this book, as you get a guided tour of Gmail.

This first lesson serves as an overview of Gmail, showing you what's available so you know what it's capable of. The actual in-depth details appear in the upcoming lessons.

Gmail has become endlessly more powerful and extended than what it was when it was first introduced. Graduating from a simple email program, it now is a rich and somewhat complex online application that does just about all any mail program could do with the addition of other gems, such as Google Buzz and Chat.

Among its top attractions is that Gmail is known as today's best spam-killer. In a day when everyone, including government regulators, seems unable to do anything about spam, Gmail turns out to be a spam-free haven. It is literally the case that you can go years without receiving a single piece of spam, something that has attracted many users.

Because it's online, you can access it anywhere you have Internet access (and now, in fact, you can use it offline to compose messages, as you'll see, and sync with Gmail when you get back online). That makes Gmail very attractive to people who travel a good deal and live in Wi-Fi enhanced environments.

There are additional terrific communications applications built right in to Gmail, such as Buzz (Google's answer to Twitter) and Chat (where you can type interactively with others). You'll see both of these in depth in this book.

Another selling point is that you never have to delete anything on Gmail to make room for more mail—you have an automatic 7.5GB of disk space, all to yourself. You can archive your mail for years and use Google's built-in search tools to search for just the message you want, whether it came yesterday or seven years ago.

All this is in addition to Gmail itself—an excellent, easy-to-use mail program that lets you compose, send, spell check, archive, organize, and filter your mail.

And perhaps the best part is that it's all free.

Let's get started in this lesson by seeing what Gmail has to offer you.

Sending Email

When most people think of mail programs, they think about sending mail, which is appropriate enough. Gmail offers you the Mail Composer to send mail, as shown in Figure 1.1.

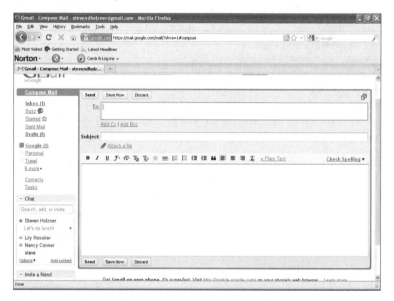

FIGURE 1.1   The Gmail Mail Composer.

The Mail Composer is central to Gmail—it's where you'll create the messages that you send. As you can see in the figure, the Mail Composer is a fully featured program in its own right, with formatting, spellchecking, and more.

At its most basic, enter the email address you want to send the mail to, the subject, and the message itself, and click the **Send** button. Your mail will then be on its way.

> NOTE: **Sending and Formatting Mail**
> Learn more about composing and sending your email in Lesson 3, "Composing Your Mail."

Formatting Your Email

The Mail Composer sends mail in HTML format, which means that you have plenty of formatting options at your fingertips when you compose mail. You can select fonts, colors, and sizes; add bold and italic; and underline and indent text, for example. You can see the Mail Composer at work in Figure 1.2.

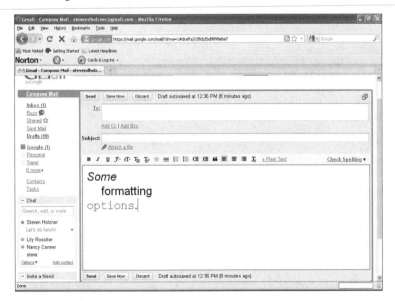

FIGURE 1.2   Composing mail.

Just because Gmail works online, don't expect any less than you'd get from a desktop email program.

Saving Drafts

Here's another nice feature about Gmail—you can save drafts of mail messages as you compose them.

That's great if you're writing a long email and need to go somewhere for a while. Just save the current message as a draft (with the **Save Now** button), or rely on Gmail to save a draft of the message for you automatically (it displays a message at the top of your mail message saying your message was autosaved).

How can you access your saved drafts? Click the **Drafts** link that appears at the left in any Gmail page, select the draft you were working on, and voila!—it opens again in the Mail Composer.

> NOTE: **Drafts and Spell Check**
> Learn more about saving drafts and spellchecking your mail in Lesson 3.

Spellchecking Your Email

You'd expect spellchecking to be available in a desktop mail program, but perhaps not with an online program. With Gmail, expect it!

Just click the **Check Spelling** link at the right above the message you're writing in the Mail Composer, and all words that Gmail thinks are misspelled are automatically highlighted in yellow. Clicking a misspelled word displays a menu of spellings for you to choose from to replace the word, as shown in Figure 1.3.

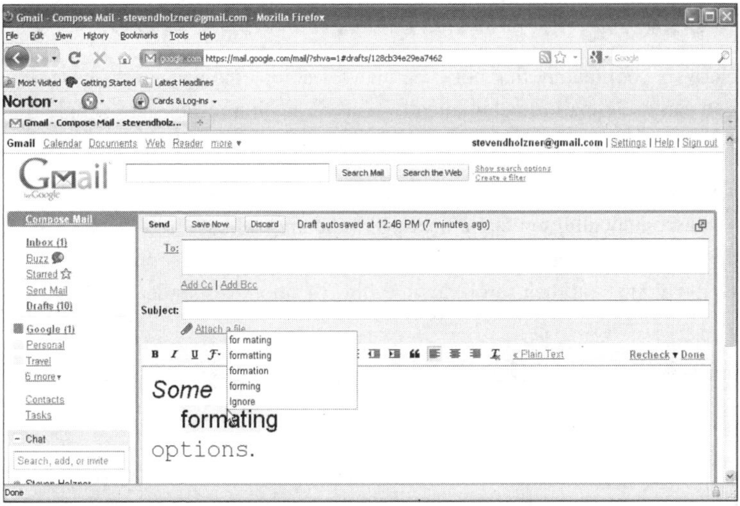

FIGURE 1.3   Spellchecking your messages.

Sending Attachments

Desktop email programs let you send files as attachments to your mail, so how about Gmail?

Sure enough, Gmail can send attachments, too. In the Mail Composer, click the **Attach a File** link, and a dialog box opens. Browse to the file you want to attach, select it, click the **Open** button, and there you go—Gmail will attach the file to your mail message automatically.

When your message is opened, the attachment will be represented as a link; clicking the link uses the browser to download the attached file.

NOTE: **Attachments**

Learn more about sending attachments with your mail in Lesson 3.

Setting a Vacation Response

Here's a cool feature that not even many desktop email programs have—
you can use Gmail to automatically send a vacation response to people if
you're on vacation or otherwise out of the office.

That is, if you're unavailable, you can have Gmail answer your mail for
you automatically, sending a message indicating when you'll be back. To
do so, click the **Settings** link at the top of any Gmail page, click the
General tab, and then scroll down to the Vacation Responder section, as
you see in Figure 1.4.

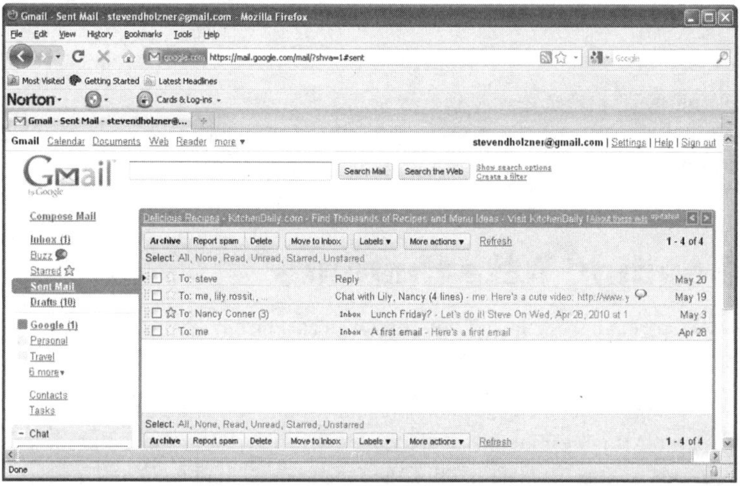

FIGURE 1.4   Setting a vacation response.

Set the starting date for your vacation response and an optional ending
date. Enter a subject (Hello from Waikiki Beach!) and a message; then
click **Save Changes** and the message will be sent to people who send you
mail when you're out of the office.

> NOTE: **The Vacation Response**
> Learn more about leaving a vacation response in Lesson 3.

Receiving Email

When you first log in to Gmail, you'll see your Inbox, which is where you get your mail, as shown in Figure 1.5.

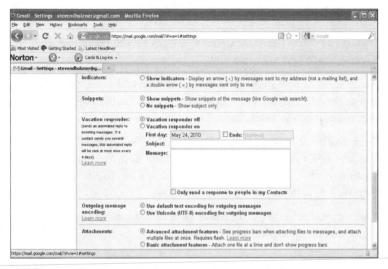

FIGURE 1.5   The Gmail Inbox.

The Inbox is the focal point of Gmail for most people—it's where the mail you receive shows up. You can see an example in Figure 1.5, where each message shows the sender and the subject. Clicking the subject of the mail opens it for reading.

One nice feature of the Inbox is that it groups responses to the same mail message together. For example, you can see numbers in parentheses following the name of the sender for some mail messages in Figure 1.5, indicating that Gmail has grouped a number of responses into what Gmail calls a *conversation*.

Note that the Inbox is accessible from any Gmail page; just click the **Inbox** link that appears at the left in any page.

NOTE: **Receiving Mail**
Learn more about receiving mail in Lesson 4, "Reading Your Mail."

Archiving Email

If you're an active Gmail user, your Inbox can get full pretty fast. The solution? Archiving your mail.

Archiving your mail stores it in your 7.5GB warehouse that's available to you by default. Messages in your archive hang around forever, meaning they're never automatically deleted as a space-saving measure.

To archive some messages, check the check box that appears at the left in each message's entry in the Inbox and click the **Archive** button at the top. That moves the messages to your archive. To see them again, just click the **Archive** link at the left in any Gmail window.

Note that you can also use the **Move To** drop-down menu to move messages from the archive back to the Inbox.

NOTE: **Archiving and Starring Mail**
Learn more about archiving and starring messages in Lesson 4.

Starring Email

There's even a mechanism for marking special messages in Gmail—you can add a star to any message you choose.

A star doesn't do anything except mark a message. When you star messages, they stand out and you can spot them at a glance. So to keep track of that amusing message from your mom or that message you want to reply to from your sister, just add a star.

How do you star a message? Select that message by checking the check box in front of the message, select the **More Actions** drop-down menu at the top of the Inbox, and then select the **Add Star** item, as shown in Figure 1.6.

FIGURE 1.6   Adding a star to a message.

You can see a star in front of one of the message in the Inbox in Figure 1.7.

Filtering Messages

Gmail gives you lots of control over your mail. For example, you can create a mail *filter* that handles your mail before you even see it.

A filter grabs only the mail you want it to grab and can do things like transfer that mail to your archive automatically, or even delete it so you don't have to. To start creating a filter in Gmail, you tell Gmail how to identify the mail you're interested in singling out, as shown in Figure 1.7.

The next step of creating the filter lets you specify what you want Gmail to do with the mail that matches the filter's criteria, as shown in Figure 1.8.

You can archive mail, star it, delete it, forward it, and so on—all automatically. Gmail will use the filter to handle your mail for you, no need for any work on your part.

FIGURE 1.7   Creating a filter.

FIGURE 1.8   Creating a filter, continued.

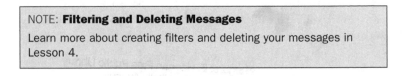

NOTE: **Filtering and Deleting Messages**

Learn more about creating filters and deleting your messages in
Lesson 4.

Deleting Messages

As you might expect, you can delete mail messages in Gmail. To do that, you select the messages you want to delete by checking the check box at the left for each message and then clicking the **Delete** button.

As is usual these days, however, that doesn't actually get rid of what you're deleting; it just sends it to the Trash. To delete the messages in Gmail, click the **Trash** link at the left (under the n More link, where n is a number) in any Gmail page to open the Trash, select the messages again by checking their check boxes, and then click the **Delete Forever** button.

In fact, many people say you never have to delete mail at all in Gmail, and with a 7.5GB amount of disk space, that could well be true. Many people archive messages they no longer want to look at instead—you never know when you might want to search all the mail you've gotten for some matching text, and you can't do that if the mail has been deleted.

Searching Your Email

Because Gmail is a product of Google, you'd expect that it would have good search features, and you'd be right. You can search through your mail easily—just enter your search term in the search box as shown in Figure 1.9 and click the **Search Mail** button.

Gmail searches through your mail and displays messages that contain text matching your search term, as shown in Figure 1.10.

NOTE: **Searching Mail**
Learn more about searching your mail in Lesson 4.

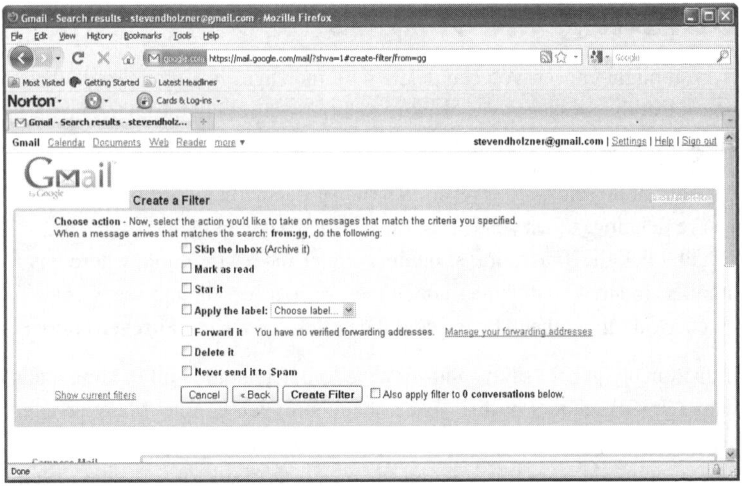

FIGURE 1.9   Entering a search term.

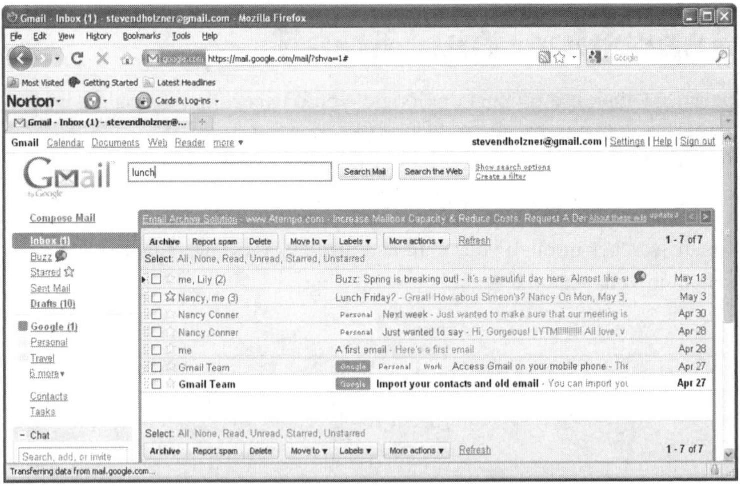

FIGURE 1.10   Search results.

Advanced Searching

In fact, you can search in an advanced way as well—just click the **Show Search Options** link at the top of any Gmail page. That opens the advanced search options, as shown in Figure 1.11.

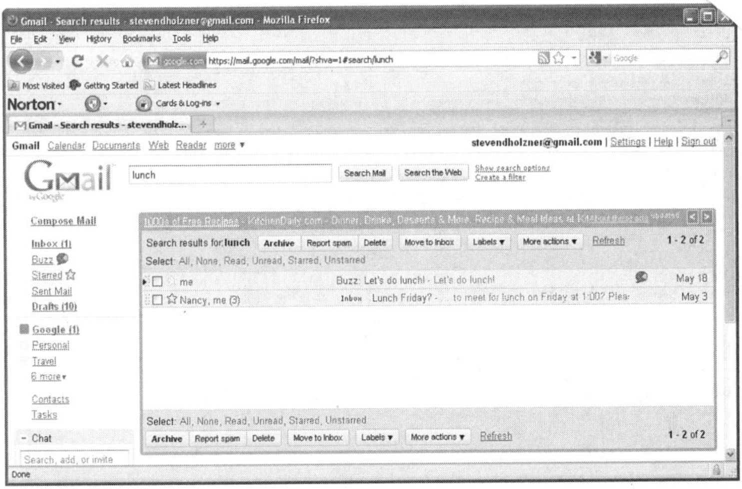

FIGURE 1.11 Search options.

In the advanced search options, you can search by:

▶ Sender

▶ Recipient

▶ Subject line

▶ Text in the message body

▶ Date sent

▶ Attachments

Gmail's search tool is very powerful. Very cool!

Checking Sent Email

How about the mail that you've sent? Many desktop email programs have a Sent Mail folder that lets you check the mail you've sent and even open it to read it if you want. Can you do that in Gmail?

You sure can. Just click the **Sent Mail** link at the left in any Gmail page to see your sent mail, as shown in Figure 1.12.

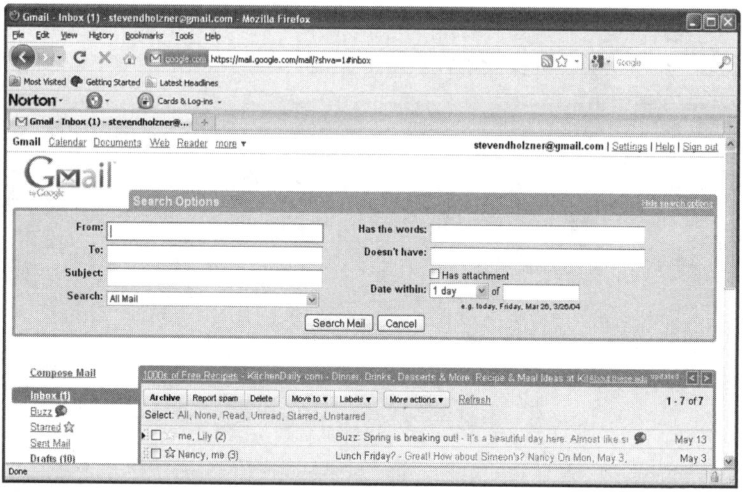

FIGURE 1.12   Checking your sent mail.

Clicking the subject of any sent mail message opens that message so you can read it. You can also search your sent mail using Gmail's search facilities.

NOTE: **Reading Sent Mail**

Learn more about reading mail you've already sent in Lesson 4.

Creating Contacts

As you're going to see, you can create an address book in Gmail—and in Gmail, it's called Contacts, not your address book. You can see the contact page for a representative contact in Figure 1.13.

If you want, you can store all kinds of information about a contact in that person's contact page. The amount of information you store for each contact is up to you.

FIGURE 1.13   A contact page.

TIP: **Fill in Those Contacts!**

Contacts are important in Gmail: the people you can chat with are taken from your contacts, and the people you can restrict your Buzz posts to privately must come from your Contacts list as well.

NOTE: **All About the Contacts**

Learn more about creating and using contacts in Lesson 5, "Organizing People Using Contacts and Groups."

Sending Mail to Contacts

Want to send mail to a contact? Just click the **Contacts** link that appears at the left in any Gmail page, find the correct contact's page, and click the email address in that person's page.

Doing so will open the Mail Composer with the To: line already filled in with that person's email address.

TIP: **Google Will Suggest Addresses**
You can also go to the Mail Composer and start entering an email address in the To box. Gmail will search your contacts and suggest email addresses that match what you've already partly entered.

Creating Groups of Contacts

Gmail also lets you create groups of contacts. In fact, Gmail comes with three built-in groups of contacts you can add contacts to at any time: Friends, Family, and Coworkers.

Beyond those three groups, Gmail lets you create your own groups, naming them as you want. You can add contacts to your groups as well and send them all mail messages at the same time.

Editing a Contact

You can edit a contact's information in case there's been a change, such as a new address. Go to the contact's page and click the **Edit** button, which displays the edit fields you see in Figure 1.14.

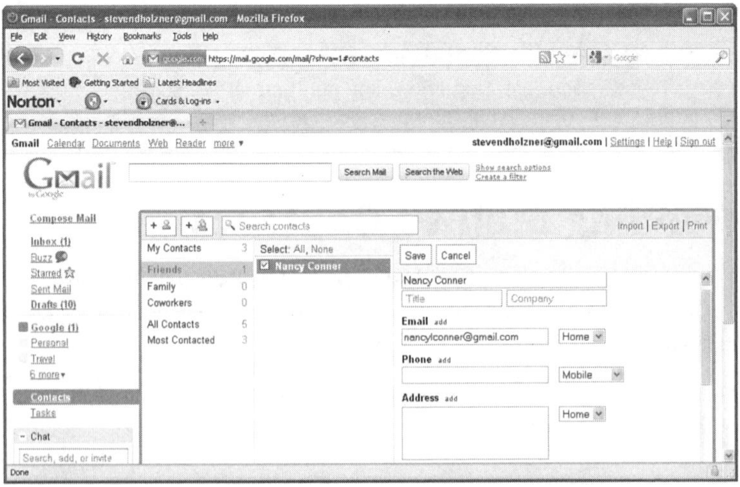

FIGURE 1.14   Editing a contact.

Just edit the contact's information and click the **Save** button to save that info.

Using Labels

As you might have noticed back in Figure 1.5, some mail messages have some short text in front of the subject, such as Buzz, Personal, or Google. Those are labels, and you can use them to mark mail messages in Gmail.

Gmail uses labels to organize your mail rather than folders. Many email programs use folders that let you group like messages together—you might have a work folder, a friends folder, and so on.

Gmail programmers decided to use labels instead of folders. You can select what labels you apply to which mail messages from a drop-down box (which also lets you create new labels), and the labels will appear at the left in any Gmail page as links. If you click a label's link, just the messages with that label are displayed, much like opening a folder of mail.

Labels have some advantages over folders. For example, you can apply multiple labels to a single mail message, whereas you can place a message in only one folder.

Suffice it to say that you use labels to organize your mail in Gmail, and that nearly all Gmail users I've met are in favor of this system over the use of folders. We'll get more into this discussion in coming lessons.

NOTE: **Labels**
Learn more about the use of labels in Lesson 6, "Organizing Gmail Using Labels and Tasks."

Reading Your Buzz

Want to read some buzz? It's simple: just log in to Gmail; click the **Buzz** label; and scroll down to see your Buzz stream, which will display your incoming buzz. You have to be following people in Buzz, or you'll just see posts from yourself.

You can see a sample Buzz stream in Figure 1.15.

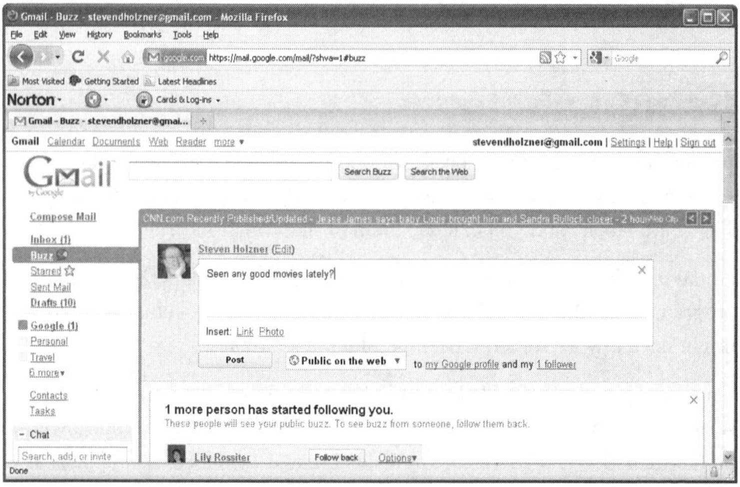

FIGURE 1.15   A Buzz stream.

TIP: **Learn More About Buzz**

Want to learn more about Google Buzz? See my book *Sams Teach Yourself Google Buzz* to learn more!

NOTE: **Getting Buzz**

Learn more about receiving and commenting on Buzz in Lesson 7, "Getting Some Buzz in Gmail."

Commenting on Buzz

If you see some buzz that you want to comment on, click the **Comment** button and enter your own comments, as you see in Figure 1.16, and then click the **Post Comment** button.

Comments will appear under the Buzz post and will appear in everyone's Buzz stream who saw the original post.

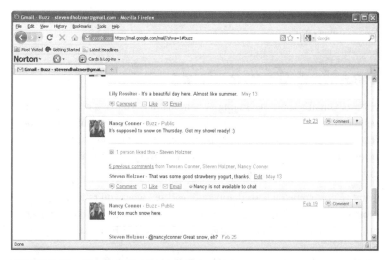

FIGURE 1.16   Commenting on some buzz.

Getting Buzz in Your Inbox

When someone comments on one of your Buzz posts, or comments on a post that you've commented on, Gmail will send you an email, as you can see in the Inbox in Figure 1.17 (note the top message, with the label Buzz).

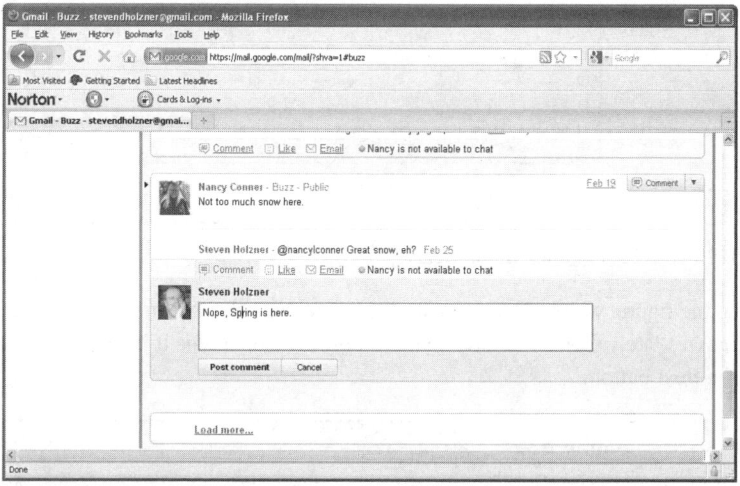

FIGURE 1.17   Buzz in the Inbox.

Sending buzz to your Inbox like this is Gmail's way of keeping you in the Buzz conversation.

Posting Some Buzz

Buzz is Gmail's short messaging system that lets you post comments that people who "follow" you can see, just as people who've signed up to follow you can see your comments. Buzz consists of fast, short messages posted and commented on by others to keep everyone current with what's going on, or just with what you're thinking.

Want to post some buzz so that people will see what you're thinking? Nothing could be easier—just log in to the Gmail site, click the **Buzz** label at the left in the page, and start typing, as you see in Figure 1.18.

FIGURE 1.18   Posting some buzz.

In the figure, we're about to post some buzz that asks, "Seen any good movies lately?" All you have to do to post buzz is to type it in and click the **Post** button.

NOTE: **Sending Buzz**

Learn more about posting buzz in Lesson 8, "Posting Your Buzz."

Posting Some Buzz via Email

Want to post some buzz via email? You can do it, but there's a catch—you have to post it from the same Gmail account that you want the buzz to come from. So there's not much advantage in being able to post buzz via email (unless you want to email your post to other people at the same time that you post it).

You can post buzz via email if you log in to your Gmail account and send the buzz to buzz@gmail.com. Here's another catch—the text of the email is ignored; Buzz takes its post entirely from the subject of your email.

Using Chat

Google Chat is also built in to Gmail. As its name implies, it's an application that lets you type interactively with other people—one or many.

Chats take place in a chat window, which can be popped out of the Gmail window to form its own standalone window. What you type, the others can see, and what they type, you can see.

Gmail also supports even audio and video chat, although that means downloading and installing some software.

> NOTE: **About Chat**
> Learn more about Chat in Lesson 9, "Using Chat."

Starting a Chat Session

At the lower left in the Gmail window (under n more, where n is a number) is your Chat list, which is a list that holds your most frequently contacted contacts. To enable connecting to a contact in Chat, you first have to invite them, as you'll see, and when they accept, they'll be made an active Chat contact. That means a green ball will appear next to that person's name in your Chat list when he or she is available to chat.

To chat with someone, check that the person has a green ball next to his or her name in your Chat list. Hover the mouse over that person's name in the Chat list, which opens a text bubble, and click the **Chat** link.

That starts a chat session in the Chat window. You can see a sample chat session in Figure 1.19.

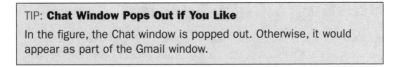

FIGURE 1.19   A chat window.

TIP: **Chat Window Pops Out if You Like**

In the figure, the Chat window is popped out. Otherwise, it would appear as part of the Gmail window.

Using Emoticons in Chat

Chat even lets you use emoticons, such as smiley faces. Just click the icon at the lower right in the Chat window to pop up a menu of emoticons, as shown in Figure 1.20.

FIGURE 1.20   Using emoticons.

You can select the emoticon you want to use to add it to your chat text.

Using Gmail Labs

Gmail has a special section of experimental features named Gmail Labs. You can see Gmail Labs in Figure 1.21.

Gmail Labs is packed with features that modify or customize Gmail in some way, such as setting the default font in the Mail Composer the way you want it, or letting you create custom keyboard shortcuts. Again, you'll get the full Labs story in Lesson 10, "Advanced Gmail."

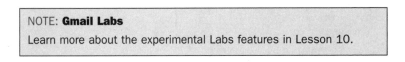

FIGURE 1.21   Gmail Labs.

With all this coming up, let's jump immediately into Lesson 2, "Signing Up for Gmail."

NOTE: **Gmail Labs**

Learn more about the experimental Labs features in Lesson 10.

LESSON 2

Signing Up for Gmail

In this lesson, we'll show you how to get started by signing up for Gmail and taking a look around.

Welcome to Gmail—Google's extremely popular online email application. This book is your guided tour of Gmail from start to finish.

Gmail is email taken to the next level—it's email made fun. Gmail offers many advantages that we'll get familiar with in this book, such as a virtually spam-free environment.

Nobody's quite sure how Google does it, but Gmail really is virtually spam free. That alone is a huge selling point for Gmail. In an age where legislators refuse to curb spam and ISPs are choked with it, coming to Gmail is a revelation to many. Imagine—no spam! I thought my ISP's spam filter was a good one when it got the number of spams I receive down from more than 100 a day to about 5, but that's nothing compared to Gmail. Using Gmail, I get no spam at all. None. And these days, that's a small miracle.

Gmail is also online, so you can check your email from where you are. If you're on the road—no problem. If you're on the road in a hotel—no problem. If you're visiting your parents—well, no problem if your parents have web access (mine don't). You can even send and check your email on your mobile phone.

Because Gmail is a Google product, all your Gmail is searchable. And you can organize your email using a flexible system that uses labels you can apply to each email.

With all this, what are the restrictions of Gmail? There aren't many. Some people may be annoyed that Gmail is online—that your email isn't stored locally. As you'll see in this book, you can now use Gmail offline, downloading your email just like any email program. How about disk space?

Does Google give you enough? Currently, Gmail gives you 7.5GB of space—that's 7,500 MB of space for your email and attachments. Not bad for free. And if that's not enough, you can get 200GB for $5 per year.

That brings us to another famous Gmail advantage—it's free. Free, as in truly free; you don't pay a cent. (What does Google get out of this arrangement? Let's not ask them—they might start charging.)

All this adds up to a complete, exceptionally powerful email system used by millions of people. Gmail is by far the most popular online email service there is. By virtue of coming with Windows, Microsoft Outlook has more users, but when people choose for themselves, they choose Gmail more than any other.

In this chapter, we'll get started with Gmail by signing up and configuring things the way we like them. Let's jump in immediately.

Using an Acceptable Browser

What do you need to be able to run Gmail? You need an Internet connection and one of these browsers:

- ▶ Google Chrome
- ▶ Firefox 2.0+
- ▶ Internet Explorer 6.0+ (Internet Explorer 7.0+ recommended)
- ▶ Safari 3.0+

These browsers will also work but won't support the latest features:

- ▶ IE 5.5+
- ▶ Netscape 7.1+
- ▶ Mozilla 1.4+
- ▶ Firefox 0.8+
- ▶ Safari 1.3+

If your browser is not listed, you'll be directed to a page that uses only basic HTML for Gmail. Here are the browsers that will cause that page to display

► IE 4.0+

► Netscape 4.07+

► Opera 6.03+

Your browser needs to have JavaScript and cookies both turned on to use Buzz (they're on by default in modern browsers, so unless you've turned them off, you'll be fine). And that's all you need to use Gmail.

Now let's turn to creating a Gmail account.

Creating a Gmail Account

Want to get started with Gmail? You need to create an account first. Doing that is easy enough and takes just a few minutes.

To create your own Gmail account, follow these steps:

1. Navigate to the Gmail site (www.google.com/mail or www.gmail.com). The Gmail page appears as shown in Figure 2.1.

2. Click the **Create an Account** button. This causes Gmail to open the Create an Account page.

3. Fill in your first and last names in the fields shown in Figure 2.2.

4. Fill in your desired login name. This will become your email name. For example, if you enter stevendholzner and it's available, your Gmail address will become stevendholzner@gmail.com.

5. To test the availability of your chosen username, click the **Check Availability** button.

   Gmail will display a positive message, like "stevendholzner is available" if your desired login name is available. Keep repeating steps 4–5 until you find a name acceptable to both you and Gmail (that is, a name you like and that Gmail says is available).

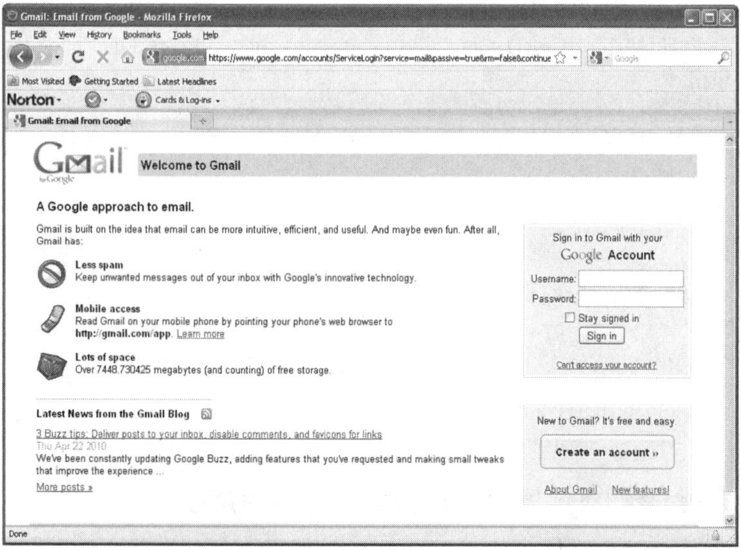

FIGURE 2.1 The Gmail website.

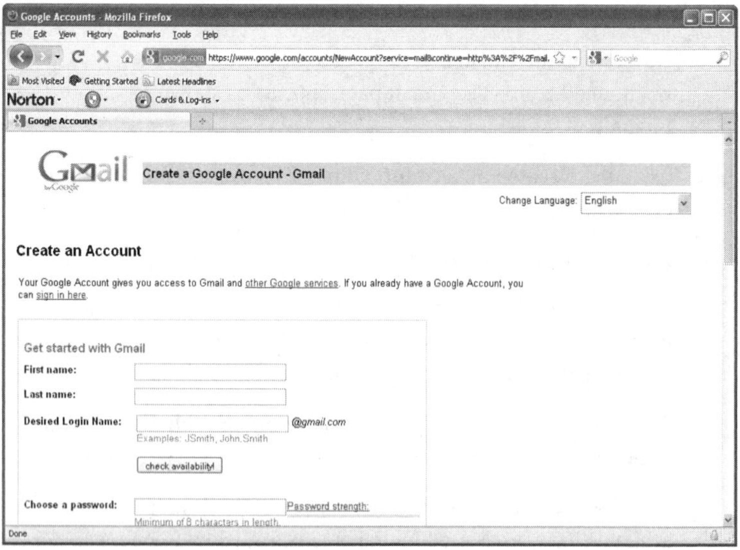

FIGURE 2.2 Entering your name and selecting a desired login name.

6. Enter your desired password as shown in Figure 2.3. This requires a minimum of eight characters; as you type, Gmail indicates the strength of your password. Include both letters and numbers for maximum strength, ensuring that Gmail indicates your password is strong.

Note that you can also select the Stay Signed In box so that you don't have to log in to Gmail every time you bring it up, and you can enable Web History, which lets Google tune its results based on your past data.

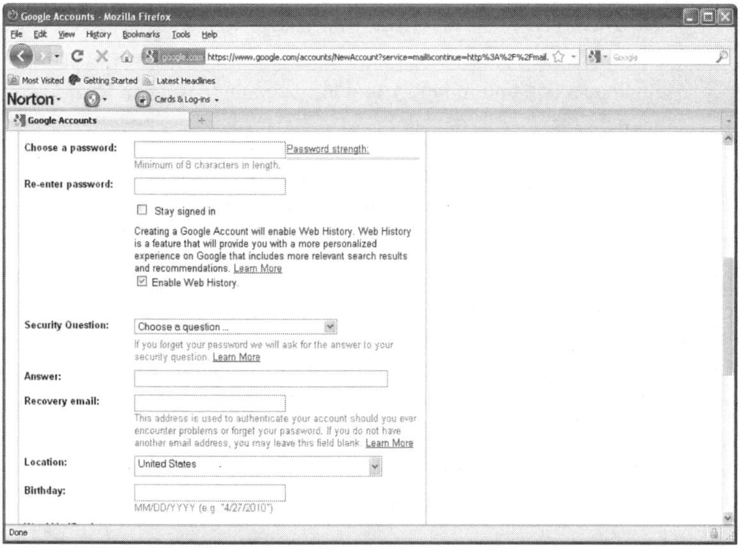

FIGURE 2.3   Entering security information.

7. Reenter your password to confirm its spelling.

8. Choose your security question. Gmail offers a choice of security questions from a drop-down list. In case you forget your password, Gmail will supply your password to you if you answer the security question correctly. Questions include what your frequent flier number is or your library card number.

> TIP: **Write Your Own Security Question**
> I don't know about you, but I don't have my frequent flier numbers memorized, and I don't even have a library card. You have the option of entering your own security question—just select **Write My Own Question** from the drop-down list. Gmail displays a text box; enter your security question in that box.

9. Enter the security question's answer in the Answer box.

10. Enter your recovery email address. This is an alternative email that Gmail can use to send you your password should you forget it. It might seem odd to need an alternative email address to get a Gmail account, and in fact, you don't need one. You can leave this field blank.

11. Select your location country. Why should your country matter? One answer is that, from time to time, Google is forced to restrict some features depending on local laws, so they want to know what country you're in.

12. Enter your birthday. Use MM/DD/YYYY format.

13. Enter the graphical word into the word verification box, as shown in Figure 2.4. Google is notorious for presenting people with hard-to-read words, so you might want to check this field first, before filling in the rest of the page, and click your browser's Refresh button to get an easier word if need be.

14. Read the terms of service.

15. Click the **I Accept. Create My Account** button.

Google creates your Gmail account and displays the page you see in Figure 2.5.

To take a brief tour of Gmail, click the **Show Me My Account** button.

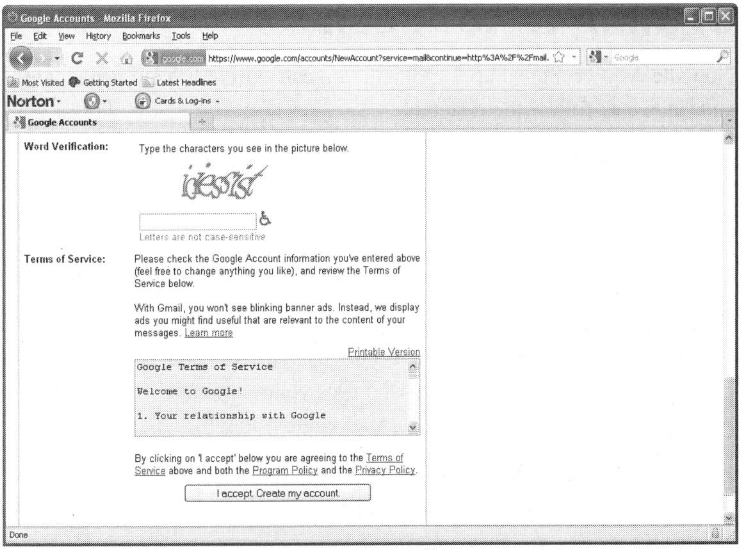

FIGURE 2.4   Entering word verification and agreeing to the terms of service.

FIGURE 2.5   Successful creation of a Gmail account.

Signing In to Gmail

Now that you've signed up for Gmail, you can sign in to your account at any time. Just follow these steps:

1. Navigate to the Gmail site (www.google.com/mail or www.gmail.com). The Gmail page appears.

2. Enter your username. This is the name you selected when you signed up; it's your Gmail address without the @gmail.com part.

3. Enter your password. This is the password you selected when signing up for your Gmail account. Be careful about this option if you are not the only one who uses your computer—if not, others may be able to read your mail without logging in.

4. Click the **Stay Signed In** check box if you want to stay signed in for the next time you access Gmail.

> CAUTION: **Stay Logged In at Your Own Risk**
>
> Choosing Stay Signed In is really convenient if your computer is in a secure location, such as your home. However, if you are accessing Gmail from work or with a laptop from say, a coffee shop, staying signed in can be a security risk since anyone with access to your computer can read your email—and worse, send email that appears to come from you.

5. Click the **Sign In** button. Gmail signs you in and displays your Inbox, as shown in Figure 2.6.

As you can see in the figure, the Gmail Team has already sent you some welcome emails to get you started.

Want a quick tour of Gmail to see what you can do? Take a look at the next task.

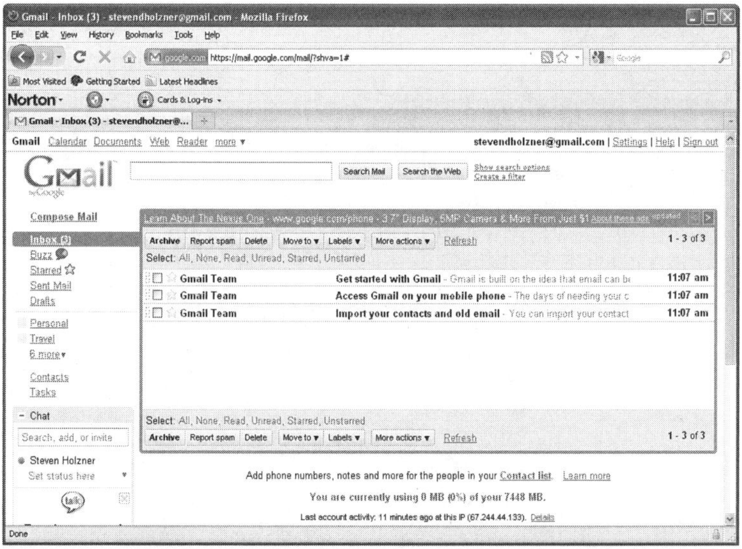

FIGURE 2.6   Logging in to your Gmail account.

Getting a Tour of Gmail

Let's get a quick overview of Gmail now that we're signed up.

▶ The Inbox—You can see your Inbox in Figure 2.6; this is a list of
the email you've received. Unread messages will have subject
lines in bold (as you can see for the three messages in Figure
2.6), and messages you've read will have their subject lines in
plain text.

When you click an email's subject line, that email opens, as shown in
Figure 2.7.

You'll get more details starting in the next lesson, and a lot more in Lesson
4, "Reading Your Mail," on reading your email. For now, you can get back
to the Inbox by clicking the **Inbox** link at the left in any Gmail page.

NOTE: **The Number of Unread Messages**

Note that the Inbox link has a nice feature that displays the number of currently unread emails in the Inbox right after the Inbox link.

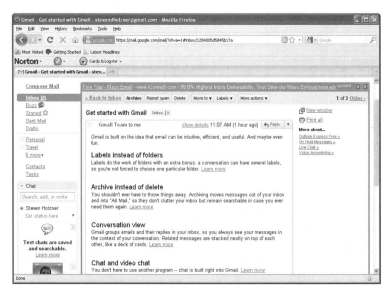

FIGURE 2.7   Reading an email.

For example, if three unread emails are in your Inbox, you'll see the link read Inbox (3). When you read one of those three emails, you can see the Inbox link change to Inbox (2), and so on.

▶ Compose Mail—To compose an outgoing email, click the **Compose Mail** link at left in any Gmail page. This opens the Mail Composer, which you can see in Figure 2.8. You'll see the Mail Composer in detail in Lesson 3, "Composing Your Mail," where we create emails and send them. The Mail Composer is an extraordinarily powerful tool that lets you write emails, format text, attach files, and much more. To get back to the main Gmail page from the Mail Composer, click the **Inbox** link at the left in any Gmail page.

▶ Buzz—The Buzz link at the left in any Gmail page takes you to Google Buzz (which is a part of Gmail). Buzz is the ultracool topic of Lesson 8, "Posting Your Buzz"; it lets you exchange short messages with other people, much like Twitter. With Buzz, you "follow" people, which means that you can see what they post to Buzz, such as short messages that can include video and photos. Your Buzz stream shows what the people you follow post. On the other hand, when you post something yourself, the people who are following you will be able to read what you've posted. You can comment on other peoples' posts, and those comments will show up in their Buzz stream as well as their Gmail Inbox. You'll get all the details on how to work with Buzz in Lesson 8. For now, click the Buzz link if you want an intro-duction to Buzz; a page appears with a video on Buzz you can watch before starting Buzz itself.

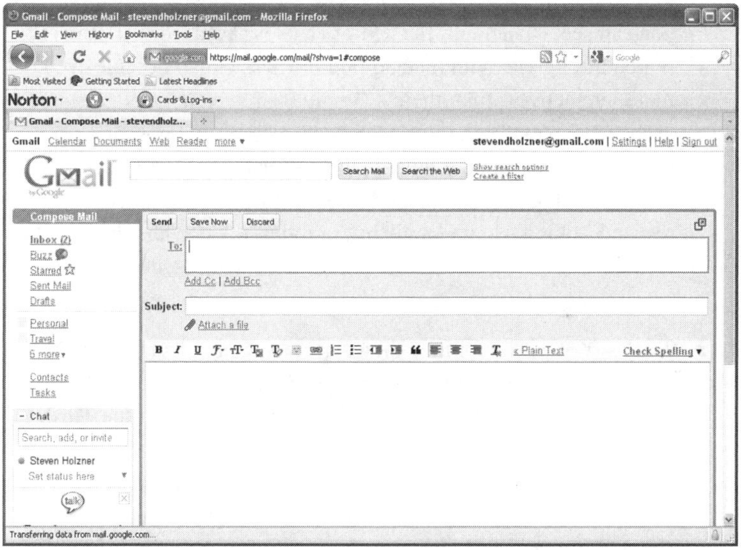

FIGURE 2.8 The Mail Composer.

▶ Starred—The Starred link at left in any Gmail page lets you see emails that you have marked specially, or "starred." Starring emails is a great way to pick out the most interesting ones, as you'll see in Lesson 4.

▶ Sent Mail—The Sent Mail link at the left in any Gmail page will display the emails that you've sent. Keeping track of the emails you've sent can be every bit as important as keeping track of the ones you get. With Google's famous search capabilities, searching through emails you've sent is a snap, as you'll see in Lesson 3.

▶ Drafts—The Drafts link lets you see emails in progress that you've decided to store before completing—that is, drafts of emails. If you have a long email you want to get just right, you can save it as a draft in Gmail and come back to it later. This is another nice feature of Gmail.

▶ Chats—The Chats link lets you chat interactively with others, as you'll see in Lesson 9, "Using Chat." Chats are real-time typed exchanges—what you type, others can see, and what they type, you can see. By default, the text of chats is saved, so you can search through it. With the addition of Chat, Gmail became even more interactive—first, there's Gmail itself, which lets you exchange email. Then there's Buzz, which lets you post and read short messages quickly. Finally, there's chat, which lets you read messages from others as soon as they're typed, and you can respond in kind. Now Google has introduced video chat in Gmail as well, where you can chat with people using the video camera in your computer.

▶ Trash—Yes, you can throw things away in Gmail, but with no spam, there's usually little reason to. When you delete email messages, they're not actually gone—you have to open the Trash and then delete them again to get rid of them permanently. But Gmail urges you to archive old emails, not delete them, as we'll see, because you have practically unlimited storage space in Gmail for such messages.

▶ Manage labels—In Lesson 6, "Organizing Gmail Using Labels and Tasks," you'll see that Gmail lets you organize your email using labels that you can add to any email. Other email programs let you group your emails into folders, but Gmail uses labels instead. You can use labels much like folders in Gmail—you can sort your email by label to view only those emails with a certain label. But labels are more flexible than folders; you can also apply different labels to the same email (which you can't do with folders unless you store multiple copies of your email).

▶ Contacts—In Lesson 5, "Organizing People Using Contacts and Groups," you'll see that your address book in Gmail is named Contacts. With Contacts, you can keep a page for each person you email frequently, including her photo and bio information. And you can email a contact with just a click, as you'll see.

Getting Email

Want to read your email in Gmail? Nothing could be easier. Just follow these steps:

1. Scroll up and down in the Inbox, if necessary, to find the message you want to read. Note that Gmail displays not only the subject of the email, but also a few words from the email itself to help you know what each email is about (Figure 2.9).

TIP: **Turning Off Snippets**

You can turn the text that appears after the subject of emails off, if you like. Click **Settings** (top right), click the **General** tab, then click the **No Snippets** option button to force Gmail to display only the subject of each email.

---

2. Click the subject of the email you want to read. Clicking the subject opens the email in the center pane, as shown in Figure 2.10.

3. When you're done reading the email, click the **Back to Inbox** link. The list of emails you've received in the Inbox reappears.

NOTE: **Bold or No Bold?**

The entry for the email you just read appears in bold before you've read the email and in plain text after you've read the message.

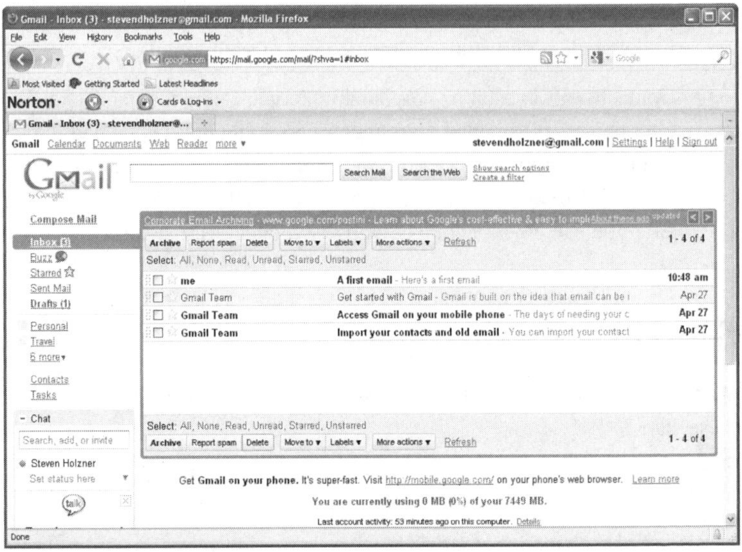

FIGURE 2.9 The Gmail Inbox.

FIGURE 2.10 Reading an email.

As you can see, it's very easy to receive your emails in Gmail. Note that if someone emails you while your Inbox is open, that message will appear automatically without a browser refresh being needed.

Replying to Email

Want to reply to an email in Gmail? It's easy. Just follow these steps:

1. Click the subject of the email you want to reply to. The email opens.

2. Click either the **Reply** link or the text box at the bottom of the message. Clicking either item enlarges the text box, as shown in Figure 2.11.

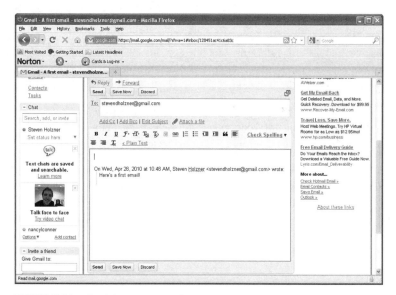

FIGURE 2.11   Replying to an email message.

3. Enter the text of your reply in the large text box.
4. Click the **Send** button.

5. Click the **Back to Inbox** link. The list of emails you've received
   in the Inbox reappears.

Your message is sent without any added advertising or Sign Up Now for
Gmail! links. That is, the person you sent the email to will get just the
email you sent, with nothing added by Gmail (that's unusual for free email
services).

Going Mobile

You can access Gmail if you've got a mobile phone that has a browser or
can run phone apps. When a feature is supported, it works just as it does
on the website, as covered in this book, but not all Gmail features are
available for all phones.

You can access Gmail via your phone's browser by navigating to gmail.
com. Do you have a BlackBerry or other Java-enabled device? Try downloading and installing the Gmail mobile app. Just point your mobile
device's browser to m.google.com/mail. Note that the Gmail app comes
preinstalled in Android phones.

You can also sync your phone's email program with Gmail. For more
information on synching your phone with web-enabled email, take a look
at your phone's manual because this process varies a great deal by phone.

You can see a list of supported features by phone in Table 2.1, telling you
what features are available through a phone's browser, in a Gmail app, or
by synching the phone's email program with Gmail.

TABLE 2.1   Mobile Phone Features in Gmail

Feature	Browser	App	Sync via IMAP	Sync via Google Sync
	Available on most devices that have a web browser.	Available for most BlackBerry and Nokia/ Symbian devices; comes preinstalled on Android.	Available on most devices that come with a preinstalled email program (Android, BlackBerry, iPhone, Nokia/Symbian, Palm, Windows Mobile).	Available for iPhone and Windows Mobile devices.
Push (Get new mail the instant it arrives, without having to refresh or check mail.)	No.	Android: Yes BlackBerry: No. However, on BlackBerry devices only, the app checks for new mail every 5/20 minutes depending on your usage. All other devices: No.	BlackBerry: Yes Palm webOS: Yes. All other devices: No. However, most email programs can be set to check for new mail every certain number of minutes.	Yes.
Attachments	View only: images (.jpg, .png, and the like) and documents (.doc, .xls, .pdf, and the like).	View only: images (.jpg, .png, and the like) and documents (.doc, .xls, .pdf, and the like).	View and send.	View and send.

TABLE 2.1　Mobile Phone Features in Gmail

Feature	Browser	App	Sync via IMAP	Sync via Google Sync
Labels	Android, iPhone: View and apply. All other devices: View only.	Android: View and apply. All other devices: View only.	BlackBerry: View and apply with Enhanced Gmail plug-in. All other devices: View and apply.	View and apply.
Offline	Android, iPhone: Basic functionality. All other devices: No.	Basic functionality.	Basic functionality.	Basic functionality.
Contacts	Android, iPhone: No. All other devices: Yes.	Yes.	Can sync using Google Sync.	Can sync using Google Sync.
Conversation View (Messages are grouped into conversations or threads.)	Yes.	Yes.	BlackBerry: Supported with Enhanced Gmail plug-in. All other devices: No.	No.
Drafts	Yes.	Yes.	Usually supported, depends on device.	No.
Storage	Minimal memory use on device.	Minimal memory use on device.	Uses device memory to store mail.	Uses device memory to store mail.
Multiple accounts	No.	Android: Firmware version 2.0+ only. All other devices: Yes.	Yes.	No.
Shortcuts	Yes.	Yes.	No.	No.

TABLE 2.1   Mobile Phone Features in Gmail

Feature	Browser	App	Sync via IMAP	Sync via Google Sync
Batch actions (Check boxes that let you perform an action [like deleting] to multiple emails at once.)	Yes.	No.	Usually supported, depends on device.	Usually supported, depends on device.
Search	Yes.	Yes.	BlackBerry: Supported with Enhanced Gmail plug-in. All other devices: Usually supported, depends on device.	No.
Archive	Yes.	Yes.	BlackBerry: Supported with Enhanced Gmail plug-in. All other devices: Usually supported, depends on device.	Usually supported, depends on device.

TABLE 2.1 Mobile Phone Features in Gmail

Feature	Browser	App	Sync via IMAP	Sync via Google Sync
Starring	Yes.	Yes.	BlackBerry: Supported with Enhanced Gmail plug-in. All other devices: Usually supported, depends on device.	No.

Setting Your Picture

When you get an email from someone in your Gmail Contacts list (see Lesson 5 on how to add people to your Contacts list), you can get a little more information about her. Just let the mouse ride over the name in the Inbox, as you see in Figure 2.12. As you can see in the figure, a box appears with some additional information, including the person's picture, if she has uploaded a public picture.

As part of setting up your Gmail account, you may want to upload a photo of yourself (this is not mandatory, of course, and if you're shy, you might want to skip this step). Doing so displays that photo to others when you send them email, chat with them, or post a Buzz comment that shows up in their Buzz streams.

FIGURE 2.12   Seeing a mail sender's photo.

To customize your Gmail account with a photo of yourself, do this:

1. Click the **Settings** link. This opens the Settings page.

2. Click the **General** tab.

3. Click the **Select a Picture** in the My Picture section. This causes Gmail to open a dialog box.

4. Click the **Browse** button and browse to the picture you want to upload.

5. Select picture you want to upload, and click the **Open** button. The photo appears with a cropping box, as shown in Figure 2.13.

6. Size the cropping box around the section of the photo you want, and then click the **Apply Changes** button. Your photo is uploaded and displayed in the My Picture section of the Settings page, as you can see in Figure 2.14 Now when people add you to their Contacts list and get email from you, they can also see your photo.

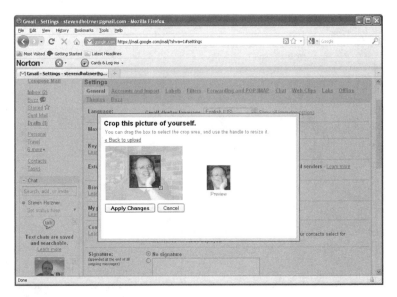

FIGURE 2.13   Cropping a photo.

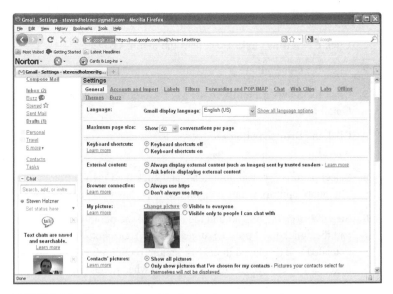

FIGURE 2.14   Photo displayed in the Settings page.

Creating a Profile

Adding a photo to your emails is a good start toward customizing your
Gmail account, but there's more you can do. If someone in Gmail wants to
look you up, he can check your Google profile, which you can load with
information about yourself if you want to.

In fact, Google Buzz puts a lot of emphasis on profiles; you can't post on
Buzz, not even a comment, without a Google profile in place. Even if it's
just a default profile showing not much more than your name, Buzz
requires you to have a profile before joining in the conversation.

Want to fill in your Google profile? (This is not mandatory; it's just a way
of introducing yourself to other Gmail, Buzz, and Chat users.) Here's how:

1. Navigate to the Gmail site and log in if necessary. The Gmail
    page appears, displaying the Gmail Inbox by default.

2. Click the **Settings** link.

3. Click the **Accounts and Import** tab.

4. Click the **Google Account Settings** link in the Google account
    settings section. Your Google Account page appears.

5. Click the **Create a Profile** link. This opens the page you see in
    Figure 2.15. You'll note that because you already have an
    account, your first and last names are already filled in.

NOTE: **To Share or Not to Share**

Note that all the additional items listed here are optional. Keep in
mind that filling them in provides some additional details about you
that are viewable by anyone. If you don't want to share this information, you are not required to do so.

---

6. Enter another name if you want (such as an alternative spelling or
    another nickname).

7. Enter the remaining personal data (hometown, current city, and
    so on) if you choose; otherwise, leave these fields blank. See
    Figure 2.16.

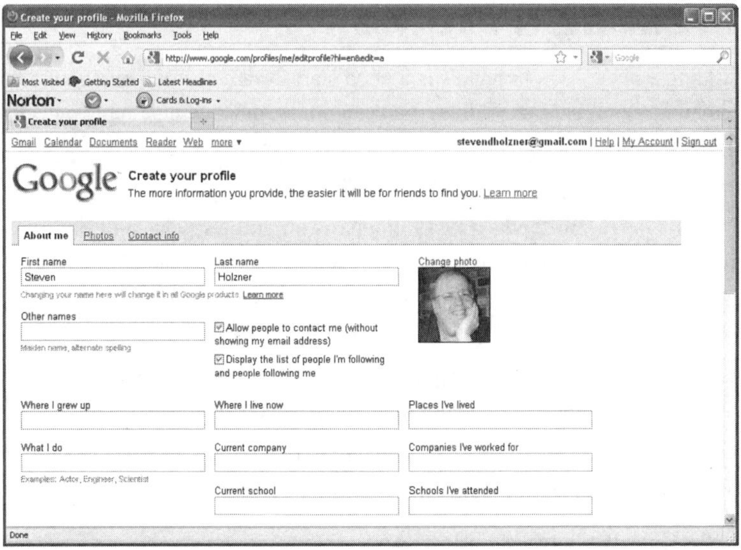

FIGURE 2.15   The Create Profile page.

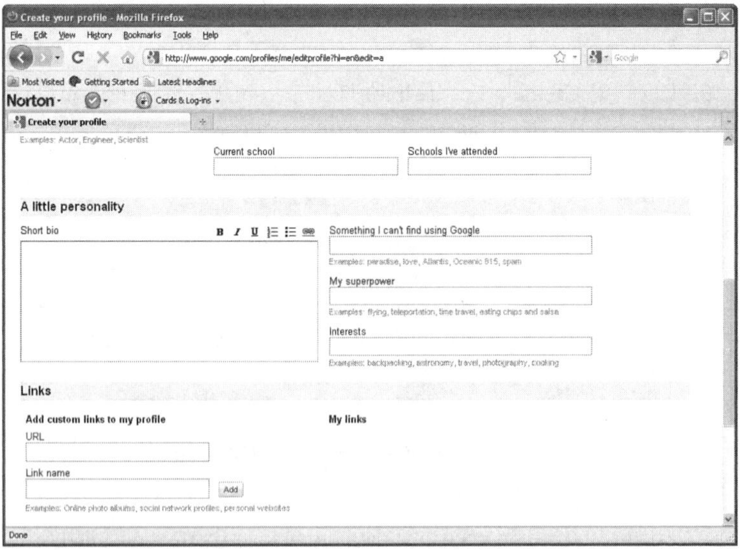

FIGURE 2.16   Filling in optional information such as your bio and current school.

8. If you have links you want to add to your profile, such as your
    home page, enter the URL in the URL box, give the link a name
    that will appear in your profile (for example, "My home page"),
    and click the **Add** button. Repeat this process for any other links
    you want to add.

9. Click the **Create a Google Profile** button, as shown in Figure
    2.17. When you do, Google saves your new profile.

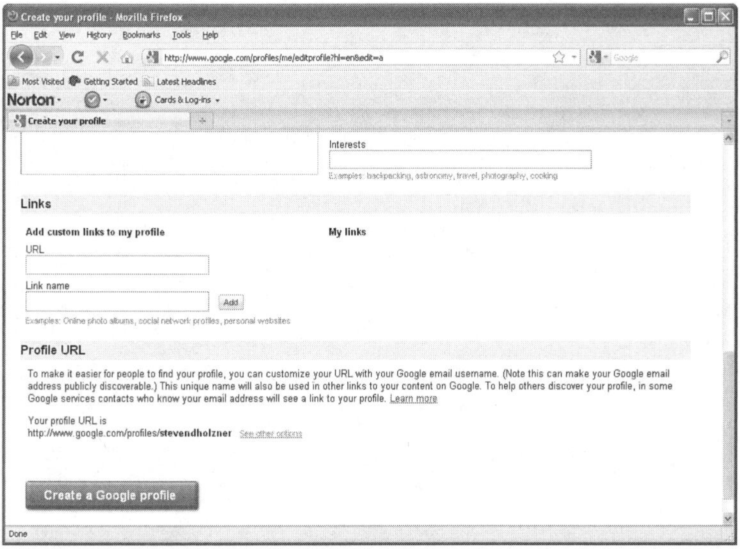

FIGURE 2.17 Finalizing the creation of your profile.

Now you've given yourself a public presence in Gmail.

LESSON 3

Composing Your Mail

This lesson is all about what most people think of first when it comes to email—composing and sending email.

Gmail's Capabilities

As you're going to see in this lesson, Gmail's capabilities here are exceptionally good (another reason that millions of people use Gmail). You can not only do all that you'd expect—create emails, format them, cc and bcc people, add attachments, and so on—but you can also save drafts of emails, work offline, and spell check your emails.

Let's jump in immediately.

Composing Email

The basic process of composing email is easy. Just follow these steps:

1. Click the **Compose Mail** link. The Mail Composer opens, as shown in Figure 3.1.

2. Enter the email address of the person you are writing to in the To box. If you want to send the email to multiple email addresses, enter those addresses in the To box, separated by commas.

TIP: **Gmail Can Supply Addresses**

If you've written to that person before, or received an email from that person, Gmail will display matches to the email address in a drop-down list box as you're typing. You can click the correct entry in the list box to select that email address and have Gmail fill in the To box automatically.

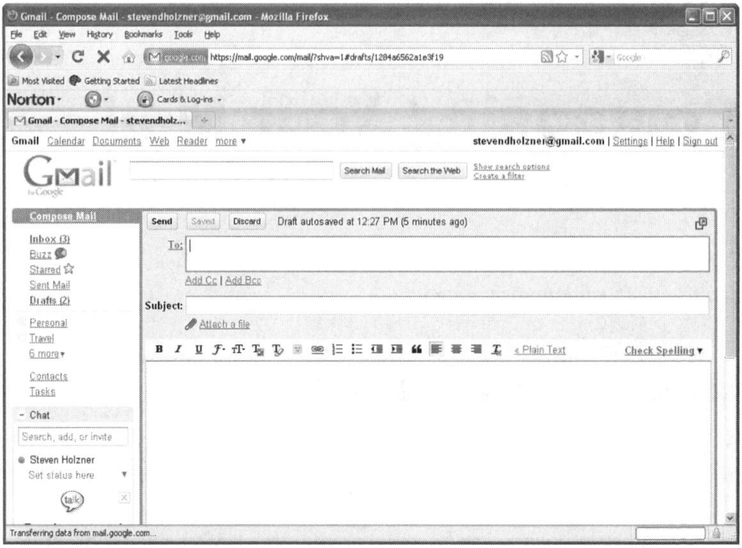

FIGURE 3.1   The Mail Composer.

3. Enter the subject of the email in the Subject box.

4. Enter the text of the email in the large text box.

5. Click the **Send** button.

And that's it—that's the basic process of sending an email with Gmail.

Spellchecking Your Email

The Mail Composer contains all the tools you'd expect, including spellchecking. You can check the spelling of your outgoing emails with just a click. Here's how:

1. Enter the text of the email in the large text box.

2. Click the **Check Spelling** link. The misspelled words will be highlighted with a yellow background automatically. Clicking a highlighted word displays a drop-down list of possible correct spellings, as you can see in Figure 3.2.

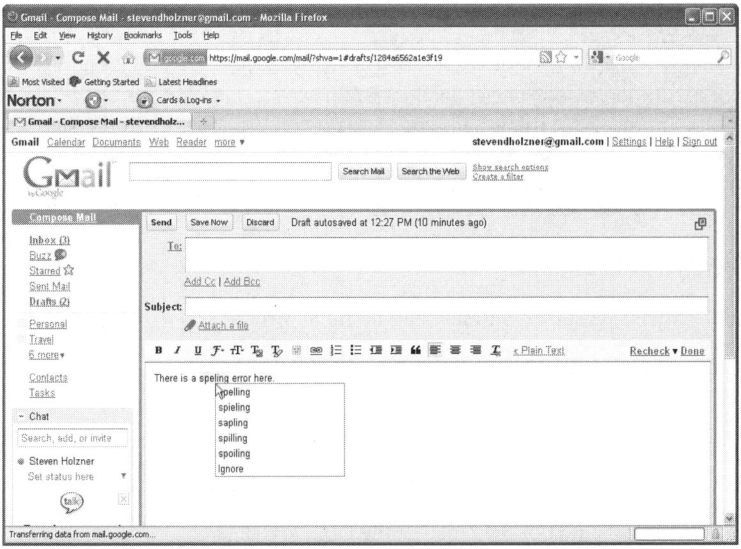

FIGURE 3.2   Getting spelling suggestions.

3. Click the correct spelling in the drop-down list. Gmail inserts the correct spelling and removes the yellow highlighting.

4. When you're done spellchecking the email, click the **Send** button to send it.

Adding Cc's and Bcc's

You can send other people copies of your email if you Cc (it means carbon copy) them or Bcc (blind carbon copy, meaning no one else is notified that the copy is sent) them. You can Cc and Bcc people when you send email in Gmail.

TIP: **Bcc All Recipients**

Here's a useful trick: if you want to send an email to multiple people, but don't want each recipient to know who else (or if anyone else) is receiving the email, put all recipients' addresses in the Bcc field. The email will then go to each recipient without disclosing that it was sent to other people or to whom it was sent.

Here's how to do it:

1. Enter the subject of the email in the Subject box.

2. Click the **Add Cc** and/or the **Add Bcc** link(s). A Cc box and/or a Bcc box opens.

3. Enter the email address of people you are Cc'ing and/or people you are Bcc'ing in the Cc and/or Bcc box(es).

4. Enter the text of the email in the large text box.

5. Click the **Send** button to send it.

And that's it—all you need to Cc or Bcc people on your emails.

Setting Text Size

You can also change the size of the text used in the Mail Composer. To do that, follow these steps:

1. Enter the text of the email in the large text box.

2. Using the mouse, select the text you want to resize.

3. Click the **Text Size** button in the toolbar directly above the message text box, as shown in Figure 3.3.

   A drop-down list of possible text sizes appears:

   ▶ Small

   ▶ Normal

   ▶ Large

   ▶ Huge

4. Click the text size you want. The selected text changes to that size.

For example, you can see text that's formatted as Huge in Figure 3.3.

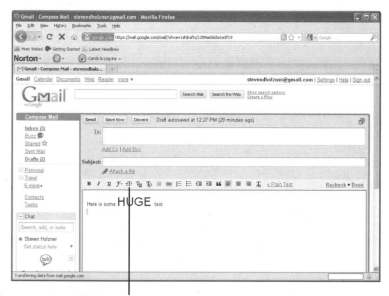

Click to change text size

FIGURE 3.3   Formatting text size.

5. Click the **Send** button to send your email.

Gmail sends your message, setting the text to the size you chose.

Bolding, Italicizing, and Underlining Text

You can also bold, italicize, and underline text. Here's how:

1. Enter the text of the email in the large text box.

2. Select the text you want to format, using the mouse.

3. Click the **Bold (caption: B)**, **Italics (caption: I)**, or **Underline (caption: U)** button in the toolbar directly above the message text box. The formatting of the text you've selected changes to match your choice.

   For example, you can see text that's been formatted in Figure 3.4.

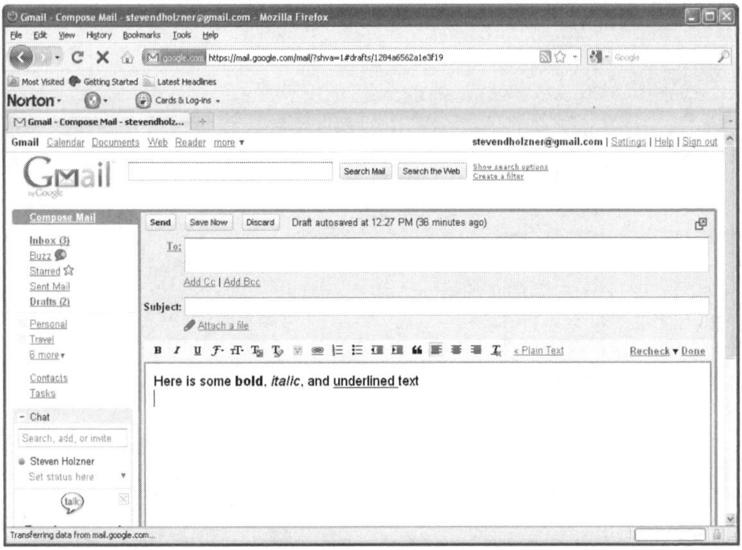

FIGURE 3.4   Bold, italic, and underlined text.

4. If you are finished composing your email and applying the desired formatting, click the **Send** button to send your email.

Bolding, italicizing, and underlining text can give your email a more polished look.

Setting Fonts

You also can select a variety of fonts in Gmail. You don't have to stick with the default (Sans Serif) font—there's a much wider variety of fonts available.

To select a font in an email message, do this:

1. Enter the text of the email in the large text box.

2. Select the text you want to change to a different font.

3. Click the **Font** button in the toolbar (caption: a script F) above the message text box, as shown in Figure 3.5. A drop-down list appears with these choices:

> ▸ San Serif
>
> ▸ Serif
>
> ▸ Wide
>
> ▸ Narrow
>
> ▸ Comic Sans MS
>
> ▸ Courier New
>
> ▸ Garamond
>
> ▸ Georgia
>
> ▸ Tahoma
>
> ▸ Trebuchet MS
>
> ▸ Verdana

4. Select the font you want from the drop-down list. For example, you can see text that's been formatted in Wide font in Figure 3.5.

5. Click the **Send** button to send your email.

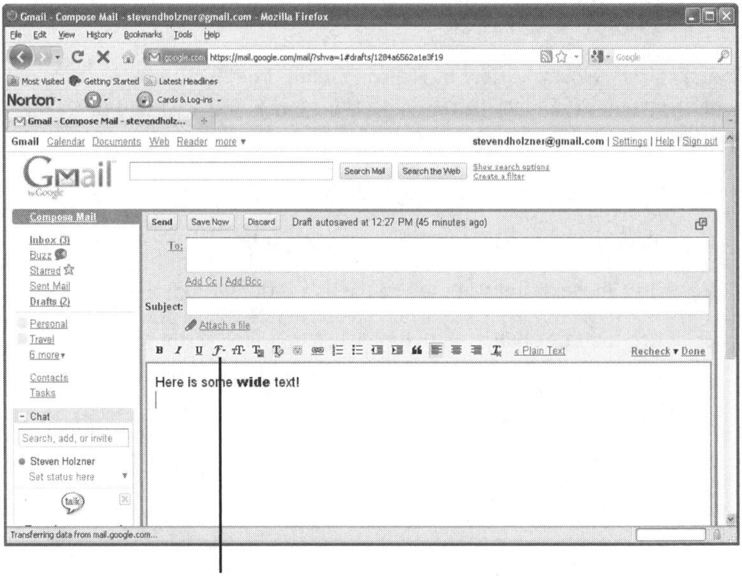

Click to change the font

FIGURE 3.5   Selecting a new font, such as Wide.

Now you're not constrained to stick with the default font in emails anymore.

Creating Bulleted and Numbered Lists

In Gmail, it's simple to create:

1. A

2. numbered

3. list

or

- A

- bulleted

- list

Here's how you do it:

1. Enter the text of the email in the large text box.

2. Select the text you want to place in a bulleted or numbered list.

3. Click the **Bulleted List** button or the **Numbered List** button, as shown in Figure 3.6 in the toolbar above the message text box corresponding to the type of list you want. The selected text is put into the type of list you want. For example, you can see a bulleted list and a numbered list in Figure 3.6.

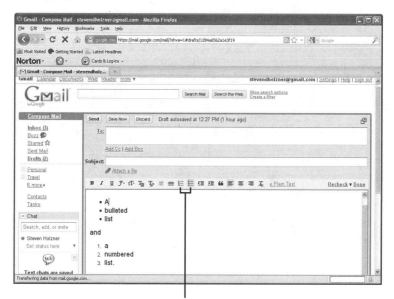

Click to add a bulleted or numbered list

FIGURE 3.6   A bulleted and a numbered list.

4. Click the **Send** button to send your email.

Now you can create snappy bulleted and numbered lists in your email.

Indenting Text

By default in the Mail Composer, all your text is aligned to the left margin of the message text box. But you can indent text on your own with a click. Just follow these steps:

1. Select the text you want to indent.

2. Click the **Indent Less** button or the **Indent More** button (both are shown in Figure 3.7 in the toolbar directly above the message text box). The selected text is indented less or more depending on your selection. However, if you haven't indented your text from its default alignment, clicking the Indent Less button will have no effect. For example, you can see indented text in Figure 3.7.

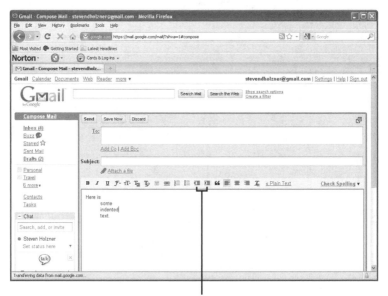

Click to indent less or more

FIGURE 3.7 Indenting text.

3. Click the **Send** button to send your email.

Now you can create paragraphs in your emails without having to use the Tab key.

Sending Links in Email

You might want to email a link to a website to friends or business associates. You can enter links in Gmail messages easily; here are the steps to follow:

1. Select the text you want to turn into a link.

2. Click the **Link** button (the icon is a section of chain) in the toolbar directly above the message text box. The Edit Link dialog box opens, as shown in Figure 3.8.

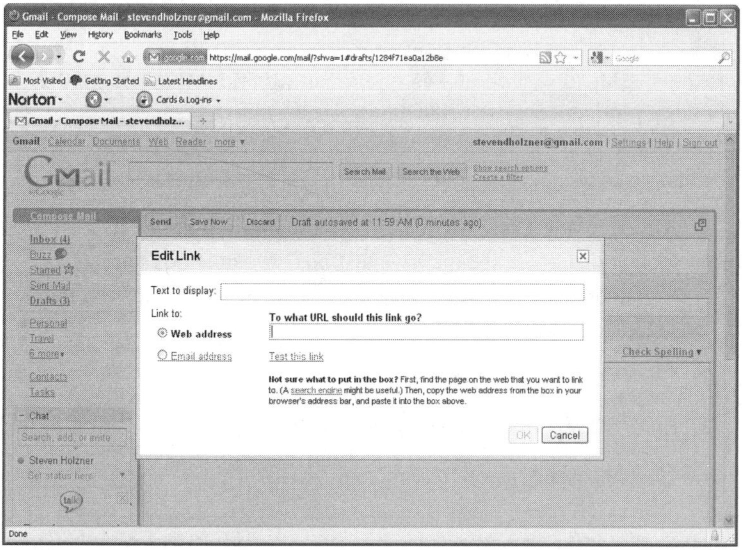

FIGURE 3.8   Creating a link.

3. Enter the URL of the link in the **To What URL Should This Link Go?** box.

4. Select the **Web Address** or the **Email Address** option button to indicate which type of link you're creating.

5. Click the **OK** button to close the dialog box. The text that you created a link for appears underlined in your message to indicate that it's a link.

6. Click the **Send** button to send your email.

Now you can send links in your emails.

Sending Plain Text

By default, Gmail messages are sent in HTML format, but at times you might not want that. For example, you might want to send plain-text emails when you know you're sending email to someone whose email application can display only plain text, not HTML.

> NOTE: **Sometimes Plain Is Good**
>
> Some users choose to send all their email as plain text because they don't always know which recipients can view HTML-formatted emails and which ones can't. Although HTML emails can be pretty snappy looking, if your recipient's email program isn't set up to receive HTML-formatted emails, the result won't be what you as the sender intended. Food for thought...

You can make Gmail send your emails in plain-text format. Here's how:

1. After clicking **Compose Mail**, click the **Plain Text** link in the toolbar just above the message text box. A dialog box appears, explaining that you will lose some formatting in the present message if you proceed.

2. Click **OK** in the dialog box.

3. Enter the text of the email in the large text box.

4. Click the **Send** button to send your email.

> TIP: **Removing Formatting**
>
> It's also good to know that there is an alternative way of removing the formatting you've added to an email message. You can select the text you want to make into plain text and click the **Remove Formatting** button in the toolbar above the message text box (this button is just to the left of the Plain Text link). Clicking that button removes any HTML formatting from the text you've selected, converting it into plain text.

Working Offline

Some people might think it's a drawback that Gmail is an online application. For instance, what if you wanted to work offline, as you can with some email programs, and then send your emails when you're back online?

You can now do that with Gmail. You can work offline, and when you get back online, Gmail syncs your email automatically, sending any email you've composed when offline.

Offline Gmail works only with Microsoft Internet Explorer versions 7.0+, Mozilla Firefox versions 2.0+, Google Chrome, and Safari 3+.

It takes some work to get Gmail to work offline, but you can do it by following these steps:

1. Navigate to http://gears.google.com/ and follow the instructions to install Google Gears on your computer. You need the Google Gears application to be able to run Gmail offline.

TIP: **Already Have Gears?**
If you're using Google Chrome, you don't need to download or install Gears, because it's already installed in your browser.

2. Navigate to the Gmail site and log in if necessary. The Gmail Inbox appears.

3. Click the **Settings** link. The Settings page appears.

4. Click the **Offline** tab. This opens the Offline tab, as you see in Figure 3.9.

5. Select the Enable Offline Mail for This Computer option button.

6. Click the **Save Changes** button. A dialog box appears, allowing you to store email offline, as shown in Figure 3.10.

7. Click the **Next** button in the dialog box. A Google Gears Security Warning dialog box appears.

8. Select the **I Trust This Site, Allow it to Use Gears** check box and click the Allow button. Gears asks about creating a shortcut for this site, as shown in Figure 3.11.

9. Select where, if anywhere, you want a shortcut to be created (Desktop, Start menu, or Quick Launch bar) by clicking the matching check box(es) and clicking the **OK** button. If you don't want a shortcut, click the **Never Allow This Shortcut** link.

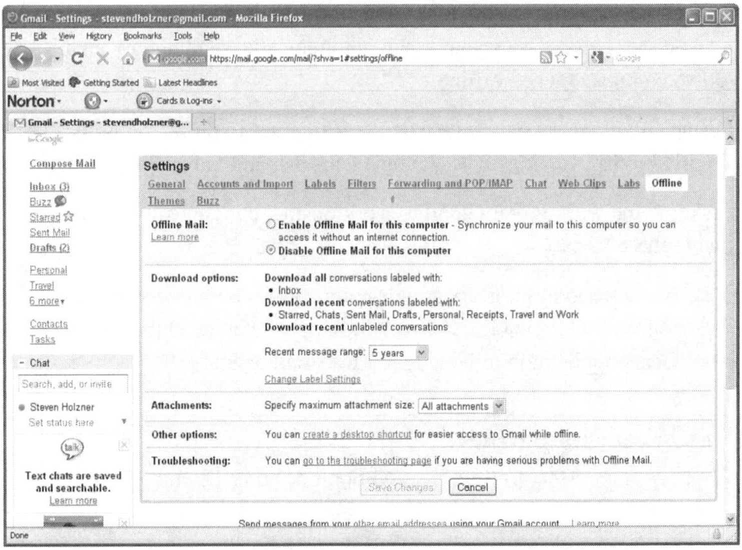

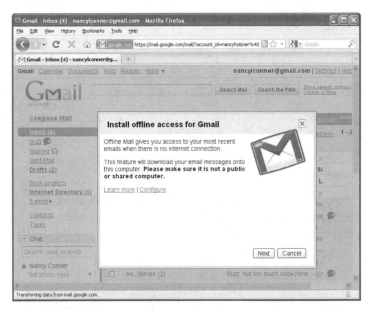

FIGURE 3.9   The Offline tab of Settings.

FIGURE 3.10   Setting up offline email.

FIGURE 3.11   Configuring an offline mail shortcut.

Google Gears downloads your email to your computer, displaying a status message as it does so. When all your email has been downloaded, Gears tells you you're synchronized, as shown in Figure 3.12 (note the check mark next to your email address at the top, indicating you're synchronized).

After your computer is synchronized, you can go offline. To work with Gmail, open your browser and navigate to https://www.gmail.com or http://www.gmail.com, or whatever is the exact URL you synchronized with. Gmail will appear, and you will be able to compose emails, as shown in Figure 3.13.

You can verify that you're offline by noting that the synchronization icon, usually a green check mark next to your email address at the top of the page, now appears pale green instead. Letting the mouse rest over that icon opens the drop-down box that you see in Figure 3.13, indicating that you're working offline. You can try to force a connection to the Internet with the **Try to Connect** link or go to "flaky" connection mode with the **Go into Flaky Connection Mode** link (flaky connections are intermittent, and Gears will try to synch when it can).

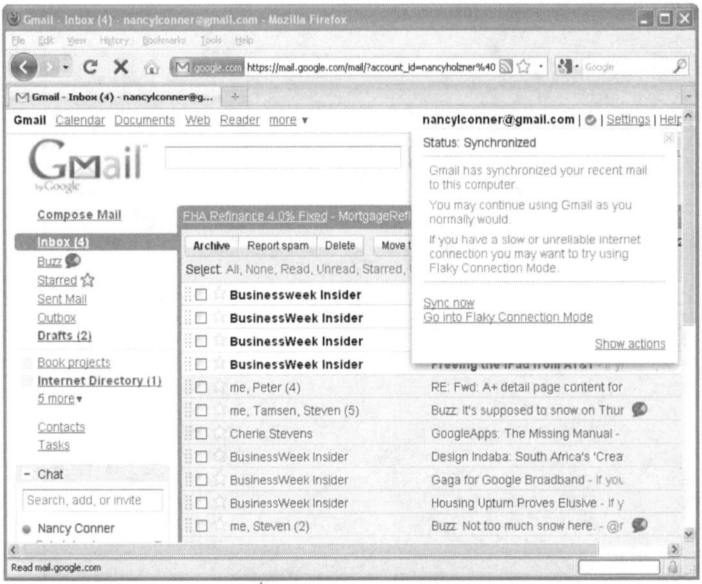

FIGURE 3.12   Gears indicating that email is downloaded.

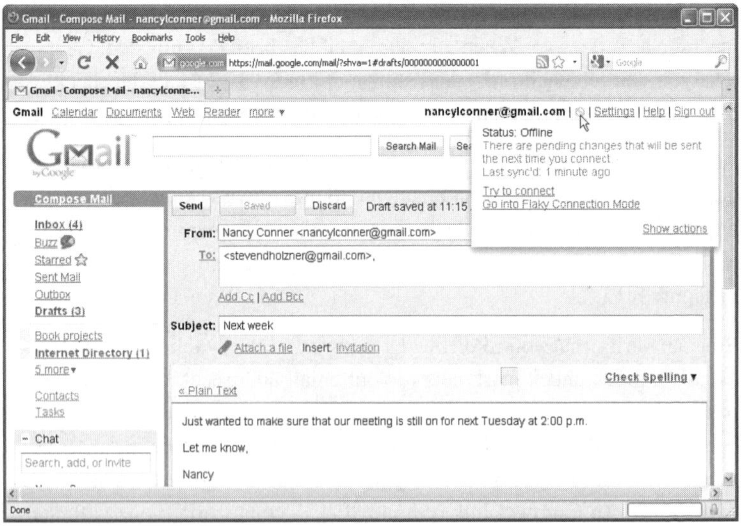

FIGURE 3.13   Working offline.

When you're working offline and send a message, that message goes to the Outbox and you'll see a notification of that with a message, as shown in Figure 3.14.

The next time you connect to the Internet, Gears automatically synchs your email—no input from you is needed. When your computer is synched, any emails you wrote offline are automatically sent.

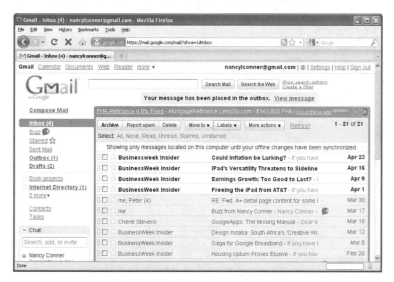

FIGURE 3.14   Your message has been placed in the Outbox.

There you have it! Now you can compose email offline and have Google Gears send it automatically when you reconnect to the Internet. Cool.

Setting Out of Office or Vacation Responses

Perhaps you're away on vacation or just out of the office. You can have Gmail send back a response letting people know that when they email you. That way, people won't wonder what happened to you if they don't get a response.

Here's how to set up a vacation response (sometimes called an Auto Reply):

1. Click the **Settings** link. The Settings page opens with the General tab displayed by default, as shown in Figure 3.15.

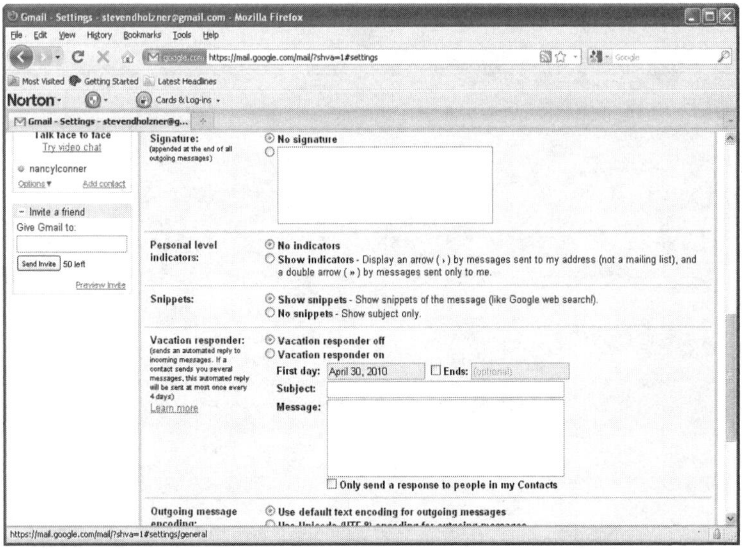

FIGURE 3.15   The General tab of Settings.

2. In the Vacation Responder section, click the **Vacation Responder On** option button. This turns on the vacation responder, which will send emails back to people who email you while you're gone.

3. In the First Day text box, enter the day you want the vacation responder to start.

4. If you have an end date in mind, select the Ends checkbox and enter the end date in the text box.

5. In the message box, enter the message you want sent to people who email you. (For example, "I'm on vacation in sunny Hawaii and you're not!")

6. If you want people in your Gmail contacts list to get only a vacation response, check the **Only Send a Response to People in My Contacts** check box.

7. Click the **Save Changes** button at the bottom of the page.

When you return from vacation, don't forget to turn the vacation responder off! Until you do, anyone sending email to you will continue receiving your automatic reply.

Saving a Draft of Your Mail

Suppose that you're composing a really long email and you get interrupted. Wouldn't it be nice to be able to save a draft of your email and come back to it at a later time?

Now you can indeed save drafts of your emails—click the Save Now button to save the email as a draft.

To access the draft later, click the **Drafts** link at the left in any Gmail page, and click the draft you want to open. The draft opens in the Mail Composer, and you're ready to continue again from where you started.

> TIP: **Your Mail is Automatically Saved**
>
> As you're composing emails, Gmail automatically saves them as drafts every few minutes. If something goes wrong, you can always go back to an autosaved draft of your current email.

Sending Attachments

Do you want to attach a file to an email? A photo for the folks, or a spreadsheet for the boss, perhaps? In Gmail, sending attachments is a snap. Just follow these steps:

1. Click the **Attach a File** link, as shown in Figure 3.16. Gmail displays a dialog box that lets you browse to the file you want to attach.

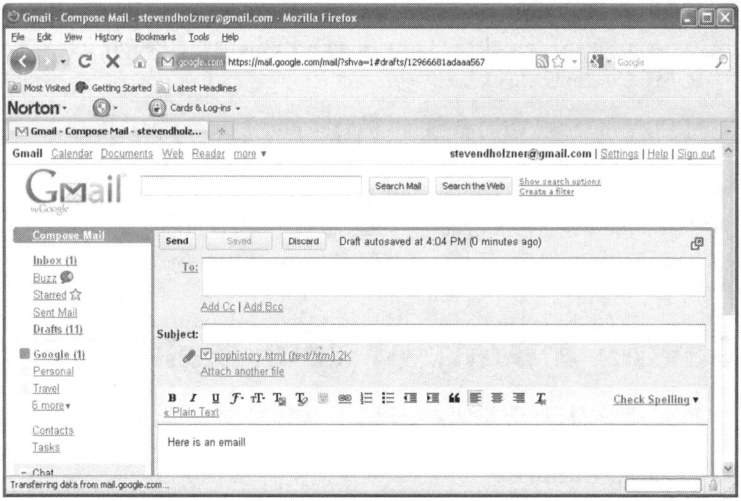

FIGURE 3.16   Attaching a file.

2. Browse to the file to attach and select it.

3. Click the **Open** button in the dialog box. The name of the attached file is displayed in your email.

4. Repeat steps 1–3 for any additional attachments. Note that the link in Step 6 changes to Attach Another File after you've attached the first file.

5. Click the **Send** button to send your email.

At this time, there is no limit on the attachment size you can send in Gmail, but keep in mind that your total disk space is limited (currently) to about 7.5GB.

LESSON 4

Reading Your Mail

*This is the lesson where the Inbox shines—it's all about reading your mail.
You'll see how to receive, read, and deal with mail in this lesson.*

Working in the Inbox

There are various ways of dealing with your mail that we'll discuss here,
such as starring important messages for later reference, reporting mail as
spam, archiving mail, and more. One thing you're not going to see in this
lesson is how to use Gmail labels. That's because that topic is covered in
Lesson 6, "Organizing Gmail Using Labels and Tasks."

Let's jump in and get some mail!

Reading Mail

When someone sends you mail, that mail ends up in your Inbox, and that's
where this lesson starts. Want to access the mail in your Inbox? Just follow
these steps:

1. Navigate to the Gmail site and log in if necessary. The Gmail
   page appears, displaying the Gmail Inbox by default. Your mail
   appears in your Inbox. New mail uses bold text for the subject,
   and mail you've already read uses plain text for the subject of the
   mail. A sample Gmail Inbox appears in Figure 4.1.

2. Click the subject of the mail you want to read. Your mail opens,
   as shown in Figure 4.2.

3. To get back to the Inbox, click the **Back to Inbox** link that
   appears at the top of the mail.

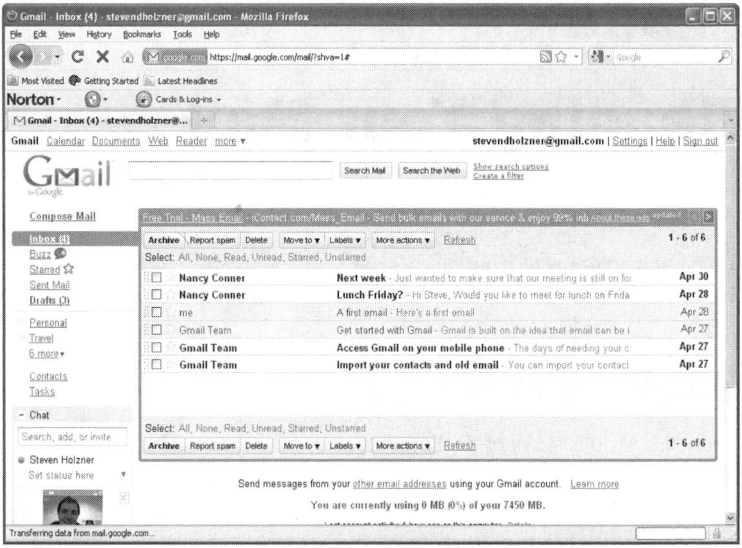

FIGURE 4.1   The Gmail Inbox.

FIGURE 4.2   Reading mail.

Searching Your Mail

Because this is Google, you'd expect that you can search your mail, and of course you can. You can perform basic searches of your mail by entering a search term in the Search box that appears above the Inbox and clicking the **Search Mail** button—matching results are displayed. However, if you want to perform more than the most basic of searches, follow these steps:

1. In the Inbox click the **Show Search Options** link next to the Search buttons. The search options appear, as shown in Figure 4.3.

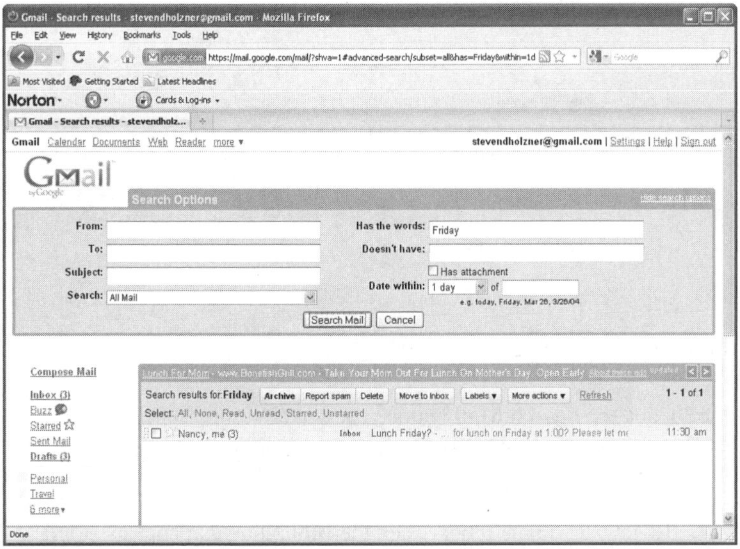

FIGURE 4.3   The search options for mail.

2. Enter the information pinpointing what you'd like to search for. The possibilities are as follows:

   ▶ From—Search for mail from a specific person.

   ▶ To—Search for mail to a specific person.

   ▶ Subject—Search for mail with a particular subject.

   ▶ Search—In this box, you can restrict the search to the set of mail you want to check—read mail, unread mail, starred mail, spam, trashed mail, and more.

▶ With the Words—Search the body of mail for specific words.

▶ Doesn't Have—Search for mail that doesn't have specific words.

▶ Has Attachment—Check this check box if you want to search only mail that has an attachment.

▶ Date Within—Search mail with the date within a specified range of the date you enter. The possible ranges are

   ▶ 1 day

   ▶ 3 days

   ▶ 1 week

   ▶ 2 weeks

   ▶ 1 month

   ▶ 2 months

   ▶ 6 months

   ▶ 1 year

3. Click the **Search Mail** button. The search results appear, as shown in Figure 4.3 (which shows a search for mail containing the word *Friday*).

4. To get back to the Inbox, click the **Inbox** link that appears at left in the page.

Displaying Only Unread Mail

Want to display just your unread mail? You can click the **Unread** link at the top of the Inbox to highlight all unread mail, which adds a check mark to each unread mail's check box, as shown in Figure 4.4.

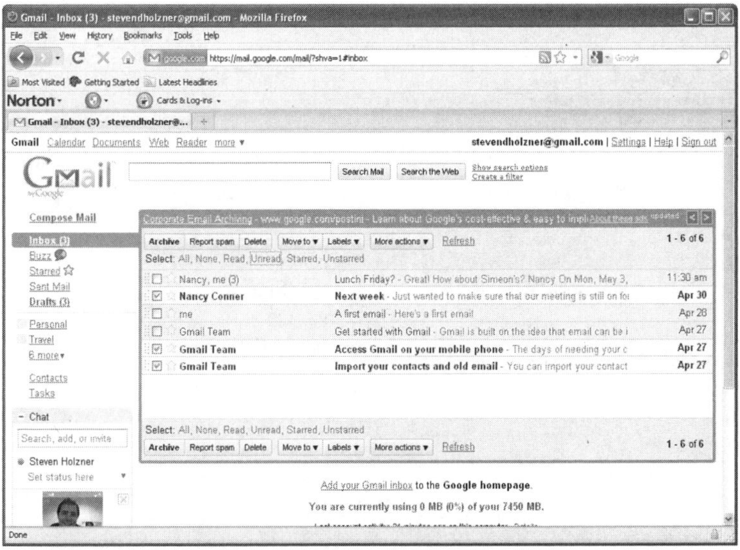

FIGURE 4.4   Selecting unread mail.

Your unread mail is selected and displayed with a yellow background. However, selecting mail like this is the first step to working with mail messages in a group—after you select messages, you can click the **Delete** button to delete them, for example.

Gmail offers only one way to view just your unread mail messages all at once, and that's with an advanced search. Follow these steps:

1. Click the **Show Search Options** link next to the Search buttons. The search options appear.

2. Select the **Unread Mail** item in the Search drop-down list box.

3. Click the **Search Mail** button. Your unread mail messages will appear grouped together, as shown in Figure 4.5.

4. To get back to the Inbox, click the **Inbox** link that appears at the left.

Now you can see a list of only your unread mail.

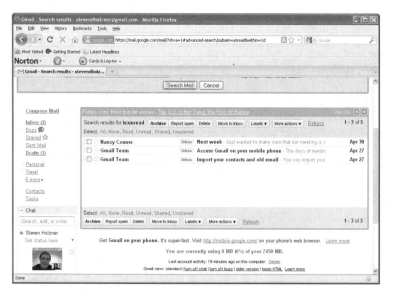

FIGURE 4.5   Displaying unread mail.

Deleting Mail

Want to delete mail from your Inbox? Here's how:

1. Check the check box in the Inbox for every message you want to delete.

2. Click the **Delete** button. The messages you've selected are moved to the Trash. The messages are not yet deleted; to delete them permanently, you have to empty the Trash.

3. To delete the messages from the Trash, click the **Trash** link at left (it may appear in the drop-down menu of the link 6 More or something similar). The Trash opens.

4. Select the check boxes of the messages you want to delete permanently.

5. Click the **Delete Forever** button. The messages you selected in the Trash are permanently deleted.

6. To get back to the Inbox, click the **Inbox** link that appears at the left.

NOTE: **Trashed Messages are Deleted Automatically**

Note that messages that have been in the Trash for 30 days or more are automatically deleted.

Want to move a message from the Trash back to the Inbox if it was accidentally deleted? Just do this:

1. Click the **Trash** link at left (it may appear in the drop-down menu of the link 6 More or something similar). The Trash opens.

2. Select the check boxes of the messages you want to move to the Inbox.

3. Select the **Inbox** item from the Move To drop-down list.

4. To get back to the Inbox, click the **Inbox** link that appears at the left.

Replying to Mail

When you get mail, it's natural to want to reply to it. Gmail makes it easy—follow these steps:

1. Click the subject of the email you want to reply to. The email opens.

2. Click either the **Reply** link or the text box at the bottom of the message. Clicking either item enlarges the text box, as shown in Figure 4.6.

3. Enter the text of your reply in the large text box, as shown in Figure 4.6.

4. Click the **Send** button.

5. Click the **Back to Inbox** link. The list of emails you've received in the Inbox reappears.

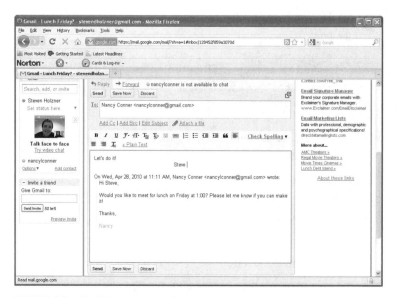

FIGURE 4.6   Replying to an email message.

That's it; your message is sent immediately.

Reading Your Sent Mail

On occasion, you might want to check the mail you've sent (Did I say that meeting would be Thursday or Friday?). Gmail makes it easy to read your sent mail. Here's how:

1. From the Inbox, click the **Sent Mail** link. Your Sent Mail appears.

2. Click the subject of the mail you want to read. Your mail opens.

3. To get back to the Inbox, click the **Inbox** link.

Now you can keep track of your sent mail as well as the mail you receive.

Starring Mail

Want to mark mail as special? You can do that in Gmail using a star. When you add a star to a message, the star appears next to the message in the Inbox, Sent mail, or wherever the message appears.

Want to add a star to some mail? Follow these steps:

1. Check the check box in the Inbox for every message you want to star.

2. Select the **Add Star** item from the More Actions drop-down menu. A star appears next to any messages you've selected, as shown in Figure 4.7.

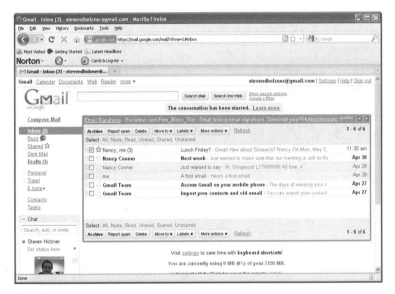

FIGURE 4.7 Starring a message.

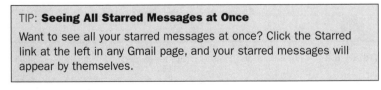

TIP: **Seeing All Starred Messages at Once**

Want to see all your starred messages at once? Click the Starred link at the left in any Gmail page, and your starred messages will appear by themselves.

Starring mail gives you a chance to make certain messages stand out.

Handling Gmail Conversations

When you send mail, get a reply, send a reply, and so on, those emails can stack up. Gmail calls those mail exchanges *conversations* (although technically even a single mail message is also called a conversation in Gmail).

Gmail has a special way of displaying conversations and of letting you access the messages in them. In the Inbox shown in Figure 4.8, the top entry is a conversation of three messages. Note that the number of messages appears in parentheses in the Inbox. Here's how accessing a conversation works

1. Click the subject of the conversation whose messages you want to read. The conversation opens, as shown in Figure 4.9.

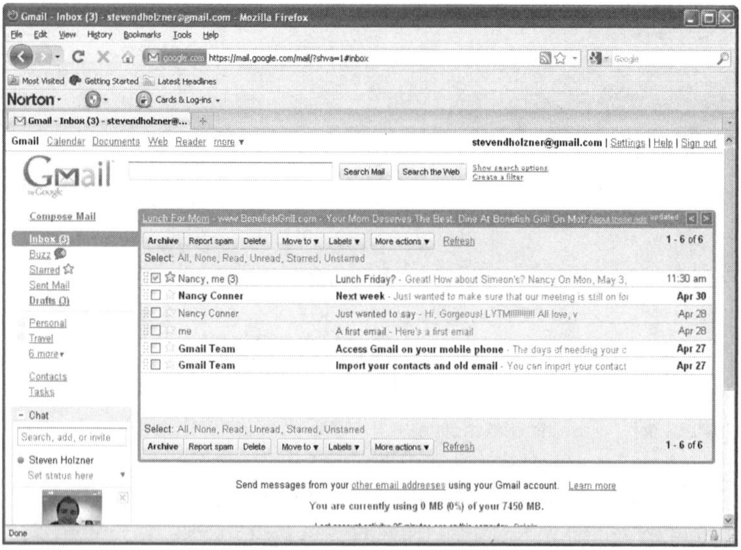

FIGURE 4.8 A conversation of three mail messages.

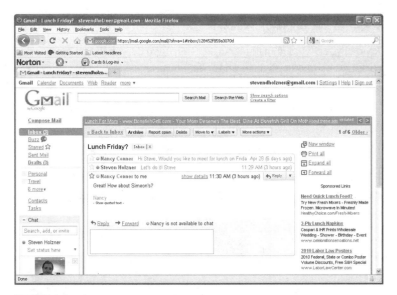

FIGURE 4.9   Opening a conversation.

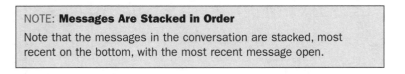

NOTE: **Messages Are Stacked in Order**

Note that the messages in the conversation are stacked, most recent on the bottom, with the most recent message open.

2. Click the message you want to see in the conversation stack.

3. To get back to the Inbox, click the **Inbox** link that appears at the left, or click the **Back to Inbox** link at the top of the mail.

Stacking messages like this in conversations keeps the Inbox neat.

Forwarding Mail

Read any really good mail messages lately? Would you like to pass such messages on to others? You can forward messages easily from Gmail by following these steps:

1. Click the subject of the mail you'd like to forward. The message opens.

2. Click the **Forward** link at the bottom of the message. The message opens in the Mail Composer, as shown in Figure 4.10.

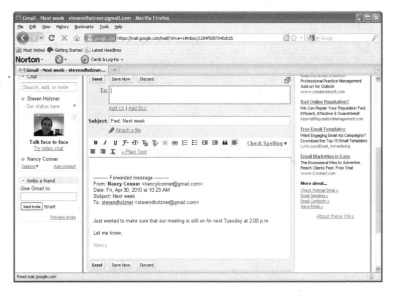

FIGURE 4.10   Forwarding mail.

Note that the forwarded text is marked with the label Forwarded message.

3. Enter the email address of the person you want to forward the mail to.

4. Enter any text you want to add in the large text box.

5. Click the **Send** button.

6. Click the **Back to Inbox** link. The list of emails you've received in the Inbox reappears.

That's it; now you've passed a message on to someone else.

Archiving Mail

In Gmail, you can archive mail that you want to get out of the way. Archiving stores mail under the All Mail link, and there's a feeling at Gmail that you never need to delete mail—just archive it. With 7.5GB of storage available to you, that might not be a bad idea. When you archive a message, it hangs around forever.

Want to archive some mail? Follow these steps:

1. Check the check box in the Inbox for every message you want to archive.

2. Click the **Archive** button. Gmail moves the message(s) to your archive.

To see your archived messages, click the **All Mail** link at the left in any Gmail page. If that link doesn't appear, click the *n* More link at left, where *n* is a number, and select the All Mail item.

Want to move a message from the archive back to the Inbox? Follow these steps:

1. Check the **All Mail** link (if that link doesn't appear, click the *n* More link at left, where *n* is a number, and select the **All Mail** item).

2. Check the check box for the message you want to transfer back to the Inbox.

3. Click the **Move to Inbox** link at the top.

Archived mail is searchable, so it can pay to get into the habit of archiving mail rather than deleting it.

Reporting Spam

I once sent a Gmail user an invitation to dinner disguised as spam ("Free dinner for two! ABSOLUTELY FREE!" and the message text had the same overheated tone until it mentioned the recipients by name and me by name, at which point the authenticity of the message was clear). The recipients opened it immediately because, they said, they never get spam, and were intrigued. So my little experiment cost me dinner for two.

The point is that spam very rarely gets past Gmail, but it can happen. If you get spam, you can report it (although it's not clear what action Gmail will take when you do). Follow these steps:

1. Check the check box in the Inbox for every message you want to report as spam.

2. Click the **Report Spam** button. Gmail displays a message saying the conversation has been marked as spam.

What does it mean when a conversation is marked as spam? All such conversations are removed from the Inbox and become accessible when you click the Spam link at the left (if that link's not visible, click the *n* More link, where *n* is a number, and select the Spam item). The spam you've marked is displayed.

Want to delete a spam message? Open your spam, check any message you want to delete, and click the **Delete Forever** button.

Want to move a message back to the Inbox? Open your spam, check the messages you want to move back to the Inbox, and click the **Not Spam** button.

Checking Your Mail

What if some mail messages are waiting to appear in your Inbox? Do you have to reload the whole page in your browser to see if anything new has come in lately?

No—if you're using an accepted browser (see the list at the beginning of Lesson 2, "Signing Up for Gmail"), messages will appear in your Inbox automatically with only a short delay. There's no need to refresh the browser window.

On the other hand, if you suspect that your browser is not displaying mail messages as they come in, or that the wait is too long, you can refresh the contents of the Inbox yourself. Follow these steps:

1. Navigate to the Gmail Inbox.

2. Click the **Refresh** link next to the More Actions link. Any new messages appear in your Inbox.

Muting Conversations

When you've got mail messages that are replied to by many people, the mail conversations in your Inbox could become long and protracted—and perhaps not very interesting because those replies may be sent between people you don't even know. This is a potential problem on mailing lists, where mail is circulated among many users.

In such cases, you can *mute* a message. When you mute a message, all follow-up replies to the message are ignored. Here's how you put this to work:

1. Check the check box in the Inbox for every message you want to mute.

2. Click the **More Actions** link. Gmail displays a drop-down list of actions.

3. Click the **Mute** item.

Conversations you mute are archived; they don't appear in your Inbox (except, experience shows, if your email address is listed in the cc field of an email—then the email is not muted).

Filtering Your Mail

Here's a cool feature! You can use *filters* to manage your incoming messages. With filters, you can automatically label, archive, delete, star, or forward your mail, and even keep it out of spam—all based on a combination of keywords, sender, recipients, and more.

So, for example, you could send all messages from a particular email address to your archive and read them when you have time. Want to create a filter to handle your incoming mail? Follow these steps:

1. Click the Create a Filter link next to the Search buttons. The filter options appear, as shown in Figure 4.11.

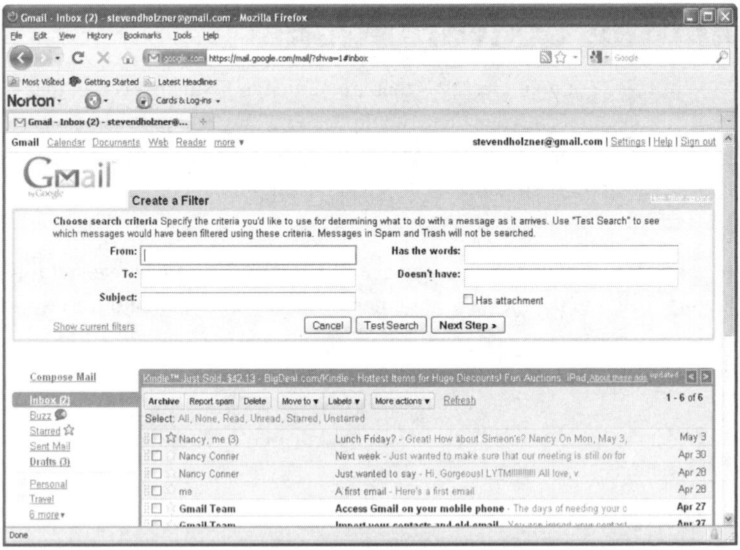

FIGURE 4.11   The filter options for mail.

2. Enter the information pinpointing what you'd like to filter for. The possibilities are the following:

    ▶ From—Filter mail from a specific person.

▶ To—Filter mail to a specific person.

▶ Subject—Filter mail with a particular subject.

▶ With the Words—Filter the body of mail for specific words.

▶ Doesn't Have—Filter for mail that doesn't have specific words.

▶ Has Attachment—Check this check box if you want to filter only mail that has an attachment.

3. Click the **Test Search** button if you want to see what mail the filter will extract from the current messages in the Inbox. This is an optional step, but it allows you to fine-tune your filter.

4. Click the **Next Step** button. The filter actions appear, as shown in Figure 4.12.

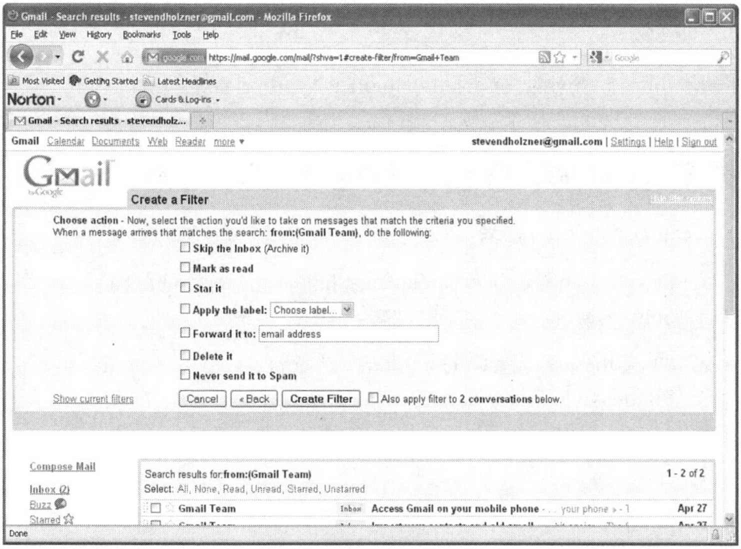

FIGURE 4.12   The filter actions for mail.

5. Specify the actions you want to take with the mail you filter by checking the check boxes. Here are the options:

    ▶ Skip the Inbox (Archive it)

    ▶ Mark as read

    ▶ Star it

    ▶ Apply the label: (Supply a label)

    ▶ Forward it to: (Fill in email address)

    ▶ Delete it

    ▶ Never send it to Spam

6. Click **Create Filter** to create the new filter and apply it automatically to all future mail. If you want to apply the filter to your current Inbox messages as well, check the check box marked Also Apply Filter to *n* Conversations Below, where *n* is a number.

Filters can be a great help in automatically handling your mail—forwarding, archiving, or deleting mail, as appropriate.

Editing or Deleting a Filter

You can also edit or delete filters you've created. Follow these steps:

1. From the Inbox click the **Settings** link at the top right. The Settings page appears.

2. Click the Filters tab. The Filters tab appears, as shown in Figure 4.13.

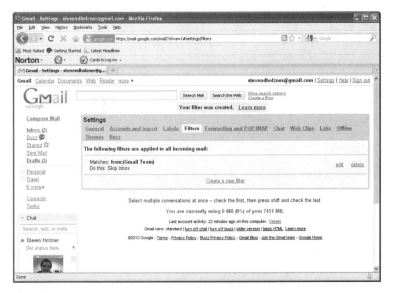

FIGURE 4.13   The Filters tab.

3. Find the filter you'd like to change and click its edit link, or click **Delete** to remove the filter.

4. If you're editing the filter, enter the updated criteria for the filter in the appropriate fields, and click **Next Step**.

5. Update any actions and click **Update Filter**.

Using the Filters tab, you can keep your filters updated.

LESSON 5

Organizing People Using Contacts and Groups

In this lesson, you'll see how to create a contact, use contacts to email people quickly, and organize contacts into groups for en masse emailing.

All About Contacts

Gmail excels at organizing, and that includes the people you email. In particular, Gmail lets you create an address book of contacts for easy access when you want to email someone.

Contacts are stored in Contacts pages, which, as you'll see, can store a great deal of information about someone. Gmail makes it easy not only to email your contacts, but also to use your contacts with Google Buzz and Google Chat.

Working with Contacts

To see your Gmail contact pages, click the **Contacts** link at the left in any Gmail page, which opens the Contacts page, as shown in Figure 5.1.

To start, the Contacts page shows a generic page. When you add your own contacts, they'll appear here, in the My Contacts section.

When you email a person, that person is added by default to the All Contacts section of the Contacts page. You can see the people you've already emailed by clicking the **All Contacts** link at the left in the Contacts page, as shown in Figure 5.2.

To view a contact's specific page, click the person's name in the center column, which will display that person's contact page, as shown in Figure 5.3.

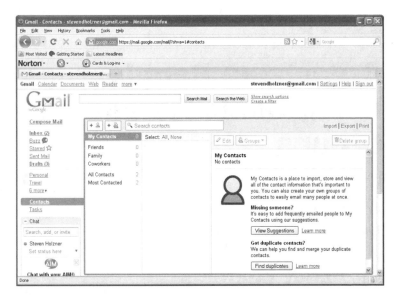

FIGURE 5.1   The My Contacts page.

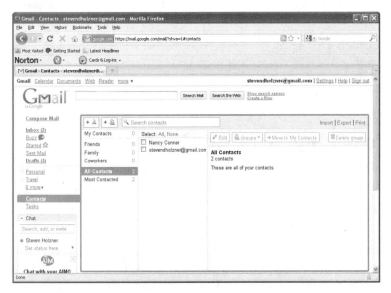

FIGURE 5.2   The All Contacts page.

Note that if the person's Google profile includes a photo, that photo will appear automatically in her Contact page. (If her profile doesn't include a photo, you can add one so that it will appear on her Contact page.)

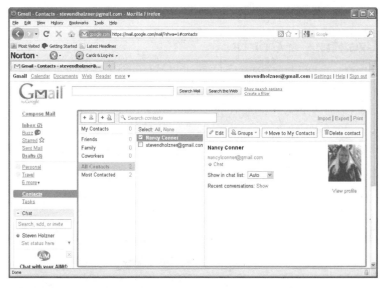

FIGURE 5.3 A sample contact's page.

Note that Gmail keeps track not only of All Contacts, but also the Most Contacted contacts—click the Most Contacted link to see who Gmail thinks you mail the most frequently.

As you can see, the Contacts pages are divided up into My Contacts, All Contacts, and Most Contacted. In addition, as shown in Figure 5.2, there are three default groups of contacts: Friends, Family, and Co-workers.

- ▶ My Contacts—These are the contacts you create yourself.

- ▶ Friends—A group of contacts for your friends.

- ▶ Family—A group of contacts for your family.

- ▶ Co-workers—A group of contacts for your co-workers.

- ▶ All Contacts—Everyone you've sent mail to.

- ▶ Most Contacted—The people you contact most often.

Note that Friends, Family, and Co-workers are groups of contacts, and that you can create your own groups, as we'll do in this chapter.

You can also create your own contacts, which will be added to My Contacts. See the next task for the steps.

Creating a Contact

You can create a new contact and add it to My Contacts easily—follow these steps:

1. From your Gmail Inbox, click the **Contacts** link. Gmail opens the Contacts page.

2. Click the **My Contacts** link. This causes Gmail to add the new contact to My Contacts.

3. Click the **New Contact** button. This button shows a generic image of a human figure and a plus (+) sign.

This opens the page you see in Figure 5.4.

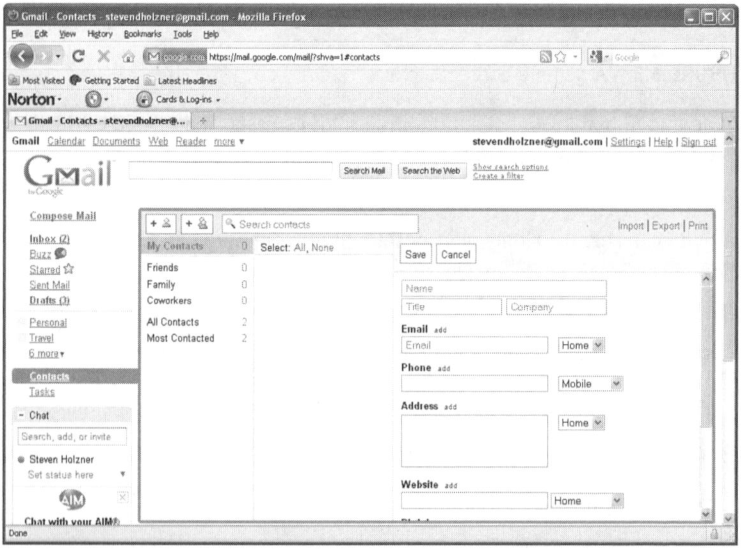

FIGURE 5.4   Creating a contact.

4. Enter the new contact's name, email, and other applicable information as desired.

5. Click the **Save** button.

And that adds a new contact to your My Contacts list.

Emailing a Contact from a Contact Page

It's easy to mail a contact—follow these steps:

1. Click the **Contacts** link. By default, My Contacts are displayed.

2. Click the name of the person you want to mail. The person's contact page appears in the right column of the Contacts page.

3. Click the contact's mail address. Gmail opens the Mail Composer.

4. Enter the subject of the email in the Subject box.

5. Enter the text of the email in the large text box.

6. Click the **Send** button.

That's all it takes to send mail to a contact.

Emailing a Contact Using Autocomplete

Gmail also makes it easy to email people you've added to My Contacts using autocomplete in the Mail Composer. The Mail Composer will suggest people from your contacts automatically when you fill in the To box. Here's how to get that to work:

1. Click the **Compose Mail** link. Gmail opens the Mail Composer.

2. Start to enter the email address of the person you want to email in the To box. If that person is in your contacts, Gmail suggests the full email address under the To box, as shown in Figure 5.5.

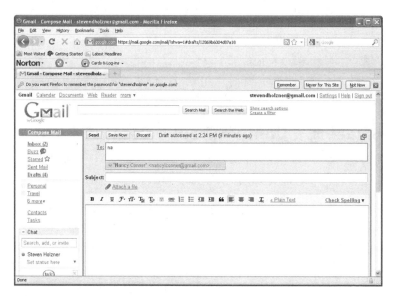

FIGURE 5.5   Autocompleting an email.

3. Click the correct person's email address as suggested by Gmail. Gmail fills in the To box for you.

4. Enter the subject of the email in the Subject box.

5. Enter the text of the email in the large text box.

6. Click the **Send** button.

Now you've sent mail to a contact the easy way.

Moving Contacts from All Contacts to My Contacts

When you email someone, Gmail adds that person to the All Contacts page, and that gives you perhaps the easiest way of creating a contact— letting Gmail create it for you.

However, the All Contacts page contains everyone you've mailed, so it can be tough finding the person you want. It's easier to move any contacts you want to refer to often to the smaller My Contacts page from the all-encompassing All Contacts page. Here's how to move a contact to My Contacts:

1. Click the **Contacts** link. Gmail opens the Contacts page.

2. Click the **All Contacts** link. This opens the All Contacts page, as shown in Figure 5.6.

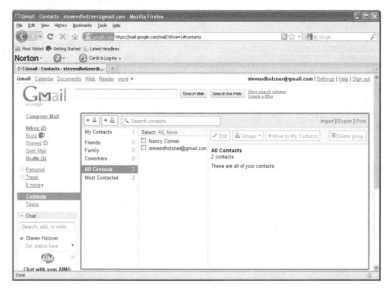

FIGURE 5.6   The All Contacts page.

3. Select the contacts you want to move.

That moves the contact to your My Contacts page, but note that if Gmail created the contact for you automatically, there's no real information about the contact in the page yet. To add that information, see the next task.

Editing a Contact

You can edit a contact's information easily—follow these steps:

1. Click the **Contacts** link. Gmail opens the Contacts page.

2. In the center of the Contacts page, click the contact whose information you want to edit. This opens the contact's page.

3. Click the **Edit** button directly above the contact's page. This opens the contact's page for editing, as you see in Figure 5.7.

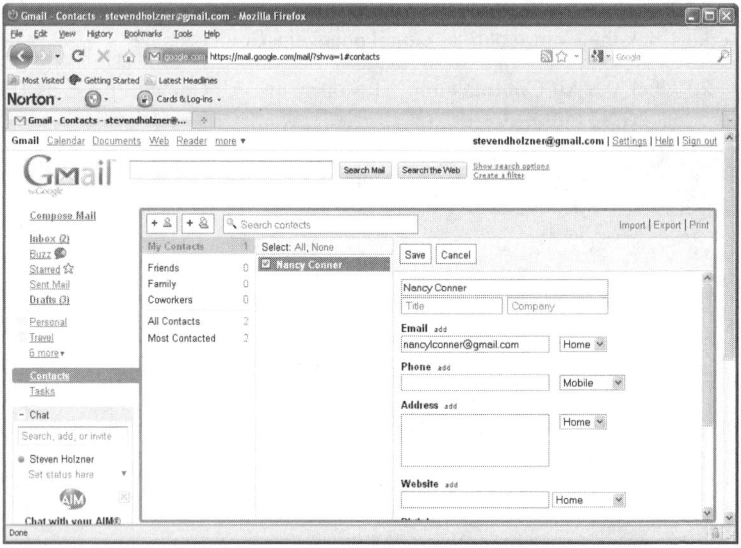

FIGURE 5.7   Editing a contact.

4. Edit the contact's information, such as name, email, and phone as necessary.

5. Click the **Save** button.

Use these steps to make changes to a contact's information at any time.

Deleting a Contact

You can delete contacts without any problem—follow these steps:

1. Click the **Contacts** link. Gmail opens the Contacts page.

2. Find the contact you want to delete and select it. Gmail opens the contact's page.

3. Click the **Delete Contact** button. This button appears above the contact's page.

4. Click the **OK** button in the dialog box that opens. Gmail deletes the contact.

That's all it takes is to delete a contact.

Setting a Contact's Photo

When you create a contact, Gmail tries to find a Google profile page for the person to take a photo from that page and put it into the person's contact page. If that person doesn't have a Google profile with a photo, you're left without a photo in the person's contact page, as you can see in Figure 5.8.

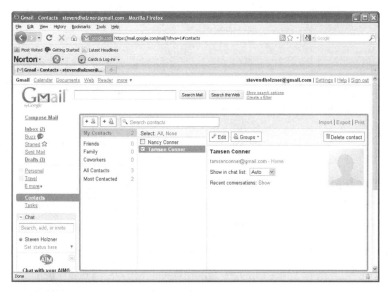

FIGURE 5.8   A contact page without a photo.

You can upload your own photo for the contact (which can lead to some pretty funny contact pages, depending on which photo you use). Follow these steps:

1. Find the contact whose photo you want to upload, and select that photo. Gmail opens that person's contact page.

2. Click the generic photo box (a Change Picture link appears). Gmail opens the photo uploader page you see in Figure 5.9.

FIGURE 5.9   The photo uploader page.

3. Click the **Browse** button. Gmail opens a dialog box named Upload.

4. Browse to the photo you want to upload, and select it.

5. Click the **Open** button. Gmail opens the photo in a cropping dialog box, as shown in Figure 5.10.

6. Use the sizing box inside the image to crop the photo.

7. Click the **Apply Changes** button. Gmail may open a dialog box asking if it should share the photo with the person you're creating a contact page for.

8. If you want to share the photo with the person you're creating a contact page for, click the **Yes, Suggest This Picture** button. If not, click the **No, Keep This Picture to Myself** button. The person's photo now appears in the contact page, as shown in Figure 5.11.

Now you can set a contact's photo anytime you like.

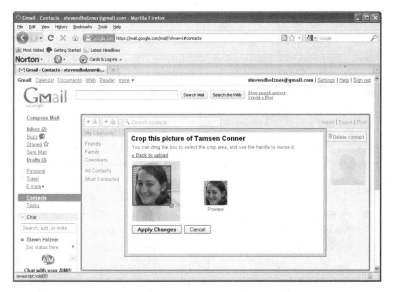

FIGURE 5.10 Cropping a photo.

FIGURE 5.11 A new photo in a contact page.

Deleting Duplicate Contacts

On occasion, duplicate contacts might end up in your Contacts list. You might forget that you already have someone in your list, for example, and add him again. Using Gmail, you can delete duplicate contacts with the click of a button. Gmail will search for your duplicate contacts, display them, and offer to merge records if appropriate.

What does it take to be considered a duplicate contact? Experience shows that even if two contacts have the same email addresses, that's not enough—they must also have, at a minimum, the same exact name.

Want to search for duplicate contacts and merge them? Here's what you do

1. From the Contacts page with My Contacts selected, click the **None** link at the top of the center column. This deselects any selected contacts, showing you the original generic contacts page you see in Figure 5.12. (If any contact is selected, you'll see that contact's page, which does not display the Find Duplicates button we're about to use.)

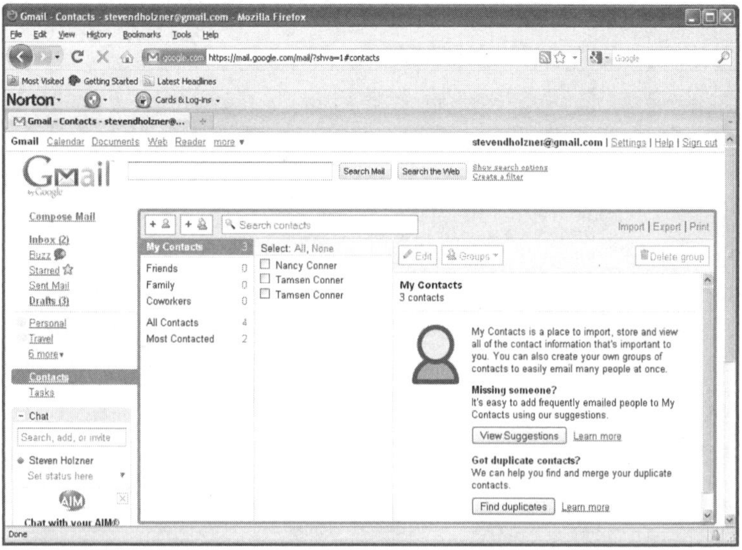

FIGURE 5.12 The generic Contacts page.

2. Click the **Find Duplicates** button. Gmail searches for duplicates
    and displays any that are found, as shown in Figure 5.13.

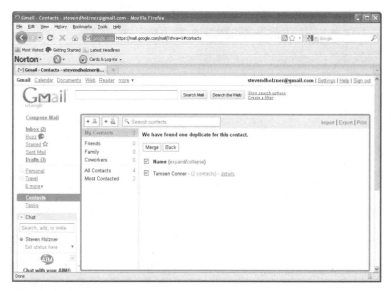

FIGURE 5.13   Duplicate contacts.

3. Click the **Merge** button to merge duplicate contacts. Gmail
    merges the contacts and returns you to the generic Contacts page
    you saw in Figure 5.12.

Getting rid of duplicates can be useful as your Contacts list grows.

Searching Contacts

As the Contacts lists get longer, you can search for the contacts you want
(this being Google, that should not come as a surprise). Want to search for
a particular contact? Follow these steps:

1. From the Contacts page, enter your search term in the Search
    contacts box at the top of the center column.

2. Press Enter. Gmail searches your contacts for matches to your
    search term and displays the results, as shown in Figure 5.14.

Note that Gmail has added a new link to the bottom of the left column of the Contacts page, as you see in Figure 5.14—the Search Results item.

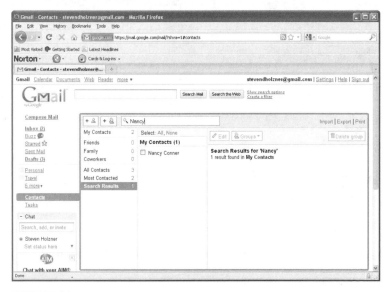

FIGURE 5.14   Searching contacts for a match.

Note that Gmail searches all Contacts lists for matches automatically when you conduct a search.

Importing Contacts

You can import contacts from other mail programs like Outlook or Hotmail into Gmail as well. All you need is to store your contacts in a .csv (comma-separated value) file (see instructions in the following section) and import that.

When you have a .csv file, follow these steps to import it into Gmail:

1. From the Contacts page, click the **Import** link on the top right. Gmail opens the page you see in Figure 5.15.

2. Click the **Browse** button. Gmail opens a dialog box that lets you browse to the .csv file to upload it.

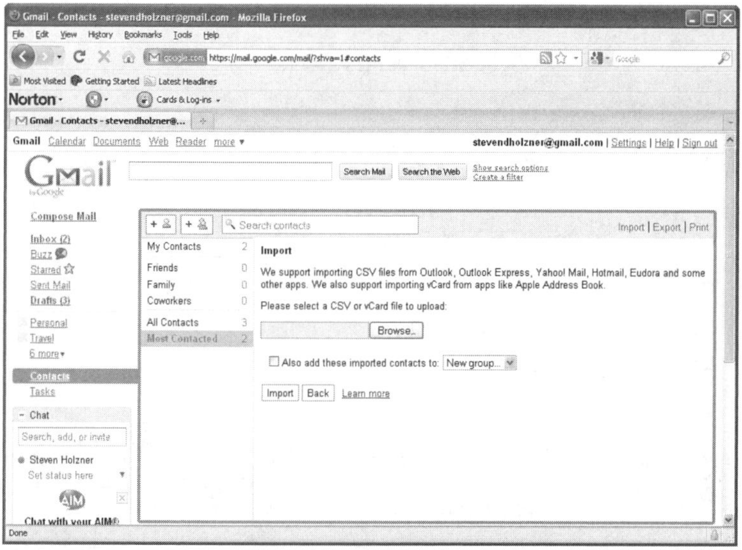

FIGURE 5.15   Importing a Contacts file.

3. Browse to the .csv file to upload and select it.

4. Click the **Open** button in the dialog box. Gmail closes the upload dialog box.

5. Click the **Import** button. Gmail uploads the .csv file and adds it to your contacts.

TIP: **Adding Your Imported Contacts to a Group**

You can add your imported contacts to their own group—just check the Also Add These Imported Contacts To check box and select a group from the drop-down list.

Creating a .csv File

How do you create a .csv file? The procedure varies by email program. Here are some directions, starting with Microsoft Outlook:

1. Select the **File** menu.

2. Select the **Import/Export** submenu.

3. Select the **Export** menu item. Outlook opens the Export page.

4. Select **Comma Separated Values** (Windows).

5. Select **Contacts**.

6. Save the .csv file.

From Outlook Express:

1. Select the **File** menu.

2. Select the **Export** submenu.

3. Select the **Address Book** menu item. Outlook opens an Export dialog box.

4. Select **Text File** (Comma Separated Values).

5. Click the **Export** button.

Here's a brute-force technique using Microsoft Excel for creating a .csv file of contacts from a Hotmail account:

1. Sign in to your Hotmail account.

2. Click the **Contacts** tab.

3. Click **Print View**.

4. Highlight your contacts by holding down the cursor and dragging it down the list.

5. Press Ctrl+C to copy the contacts.

6. Open Microsoft Excel.

7. Select cell A1 in Excel.

8. Press Ctrl+V to paste the contacts into Excel.

9. Select the **File** menu.

10. Select the **Save As** menu item. A Save As dialog box appears.

11. Select the CSV (comma-delimited) file type.

12. Enter the name you want to save the .csv file under.

13. Click **Save**.

Here's what to do it with Hotmail Live:

1. Sign in to your Hotmail account.

2. Click **Contact List** on the left.

3. Click the **Manage** drop-down menu at the top of the Contacts list.

4. Select the **Export** item. The Export page appears.

5. Click the **Export Contacts** button.

6. When prompted to open or save the file, click **Save**.

7. Select a location to save the file, and click **Save**.

Using Existing Groups

Gmail comes with some built-in groups that you can use to organize your contact. You can add your contacts to any of the three existing Gmail groups:

► Friends

► Family

► Co-workers

Adding contacts to a group makes it simple to email all those contacts at once. Want to add a contact to an existing group? Follow these steps:

1. From the Contacts page, select the contact you want to add to an existing group, opening that person's Contact page.

2. Click the **Groups** button. A drop-down list appears.

3. Select the preexisting group you want to add the contact to. For example, a contact was added to the Friends group in Figure 5.16.

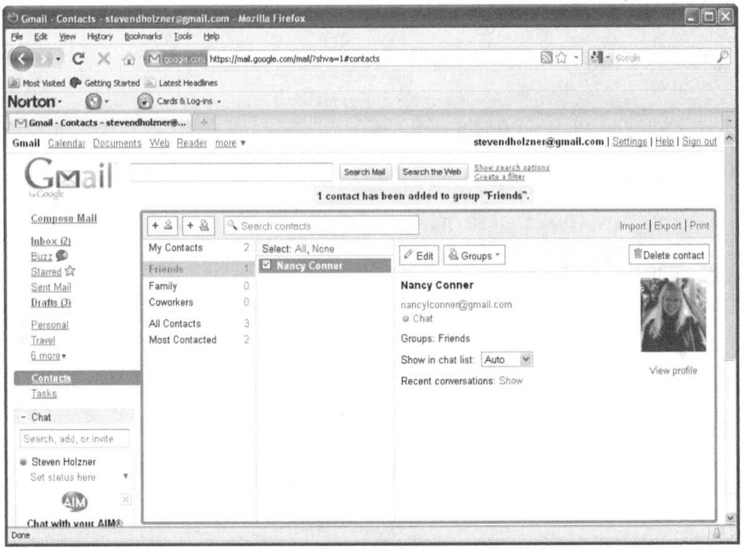

FIGURE 5.16   Adding a contact to a group.

Note that adding a contact to a group does not remove that contact from
My Contacts or All Contacts.

Creating a Group

You can create your own groups if the preexisting groups don't work for
you. For example, you might want to create a group for your comic book
club or a fund drive's members.

Here's how to create your own group:

1. From the Contacts page, click the **New Group** button (that's the
   button displaying two generic human figures and a plus [+] sign).
   A dialog box opens.

2. Enter the name of the new group in the dialog box.

3. Click the **OK** button in the dialog box. The new group is created
   and added to the list of groups in the contacts page.

Creating your own custom groups is great for organizing your contacts as you get more and more contacts over time.

> TIP: **Creating Group Profiles**
> You can even create your own Google profile for your own custom groups.

Emailing a Group

You can email all the members of a group at once—follow these steps:

1. From the Inbox click the **Compose Mail** link. Gmail opens the Mail Composer.

2. Start to enter the group's name to mail in the To box. If that group is in your contacts, Gmail suggests the group's full name under the To box, as shown in Figure 5.17.

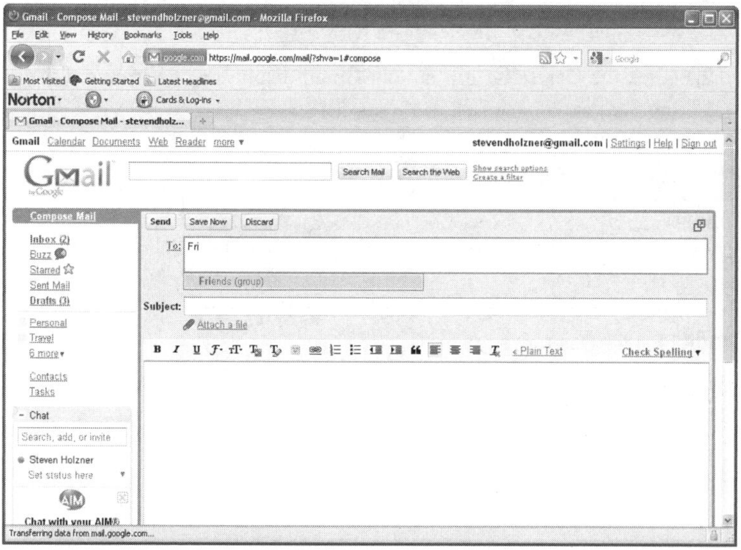

FIGURE 5.17   Autocompleting a group name.

3. Click the correct group name as suggested by Gmail. Gmail fills in the To box for you.

4. Enter the subject of the email in the Subject box.

5. Enter the text of the email in the large text box.

6. Click the **Send** button.

Now you've sent mail to all the members of a group the easy way.

Deleting a Group

Suppose that one of your Gmail groups has outlived its usefulness. For example, you may have put together a temporary group to mail people about some big event and now you want to get rid of the group. How can you do that?

Follow these steps:

1. From the Contacts page, select the group you want to delete in the left column of the Contacts page.

2. Click the **Delete Group** button. Gmail displays a confirming dialog box, as you can see in Figure 5.18.

The page at https://mail.google.com says:

Are you sure you want to delete the group Big Event? This action cannot be undone.

OK   Cancel

FIGURE 5.18   Deleting a group.

3. Click **OK**. Gmail deletes the group you selected.

LESSON 6

Organizing Gmail Using Labels and Tasks

In this lesson, you'll learn how to organize Gmail.

As you may know, some email programs let you create folders to organize your email. As a result you might have spam folders, junk folders, and work-related folders. Gmail does things differently.

Gmail uses labels. A label is a one- or two-word text annotation you can add to emails, and then you can organize your emails by label.

Using labels has the advantage over folders in that you can do everything (labeling and sorting and so on) in the Inbox and don't have to remember which folder you placed a piece of mail in. You can also apply multiple labels to the same message, whereas you couldn't share it between multiple folders.

Gmail also supports tasks. Tasks are designed to let you keep track of the things you need to do. For example, you can create lists of items, set due dates and notes, and even add Gmail messages directly to Tasks.

We'll get the full story on labels and tasks in this lesson—starting with labels.

Using Labels

When Gmail was created, Google programmers had to choose between two mechanisms for letting you organize your mail—folders or labels. Many people expected Google to choose folders because you can move messages into various folders, and that's the usual way of organizing mail. However, Google chose labels instead because it believes that labels offer all the advantages of folders and more.

After you've created a label, you can view all the messages with that label either by searching or by clicking the label name along the left side of any Gmail page. In that way, using labels is as convenient as using folders.

But you can apply multiple labels to the same message—something you can't do with folders; that is, when you put a message into a folder, it goes there and disappears from view until you open the folder. But you can apply multiple labels to the same message and the message won't move anywhere.

Next, let's take a look at how to work with labels in Gmail.

Applying Labels to Messages

It's easy to add labels to messages. Just follow these steps:

1. From the Gmail Inbox, check the check boxes at the left of each email you want to give the same label to.

2. Click the **Labels** button in the Inbox. A drop-down menu appears with these items:

   ▶ Personal

   ▶ Receipts

   ▶ Travel

   ▶ Work

   ▶ Create New

   ▶ Manage Labels

3. If you want to use one of the predefined labels (Personal, Receipts, Travel, or Work), select the corresponding menu item and click **Apply**.

   The label you chose is applied to the messages you selected. Want proof? Click the label name at the left in the Gmail page (you might have to open the **n More** link, where *n* is a number, to see the label). When you do, the messages tagged with that label appear all at once, as you can see in Figure 6.1 (that's how you view all messages with the same label).

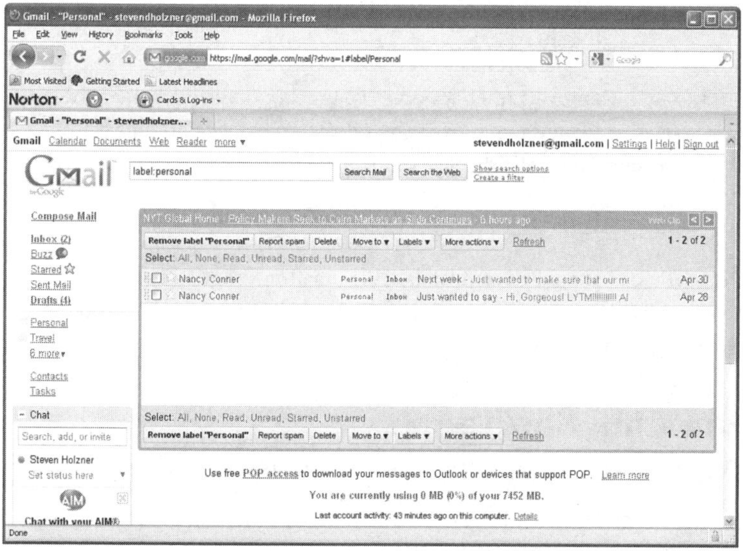

FIGURE 6.1   Emails marked with the Personal label.

The label will also appear in each tagged message's Inbox entry, in small text just in front of the Subject text.

Want to remove a label? See the next task for the details.

TIP: **Dragging a Message to a Label**
You can also drag a message to a label's name at the left to move that message to a label.

Removing Labels from Messages

Now that you've seen how to add a label to a mail message in the previous task, what about removing that label from the message? Just follow these steps:

1. Click the link at left corresponding to the label you want to remove from some messages. Gmail displays all the messages with that label (refer to Figure 6.1).

2. Check the check box in front of all messages you want to remove the label from.

3. Click **Remove Label 'xxxxxx'** where xxxxxx is the name of the label you want to remove. The selected messages disappear from the current label's display window.

4. To return to the Inbox, click the **Inbox** link at the left in the page.

Now you can apply and remove labels to mail messages—but only pre-existing labels such as Personal and Travel. What about creating your own labels? See the next task.

Creating New Labels

Want to create your own labels? Follow these steps:

1. Check the check boxes at the left of each email in the Inbox you want to give the new label to.

2. Click the **Labels** button. A drop-down menu appears with these items:

    ▶ Personal

    ▶ Receipts

    ▶ Travel

    ▶ Work

    ▶ Create New

    ▶ Manage Labels

3. If you want to create a new label, click the **Create New** menu item, enter the text of the label in the dialog box that opens, and click **OK**.

    The new label appears at the left, as shown in Figure 6.2, where the label Google has been added to two messages.

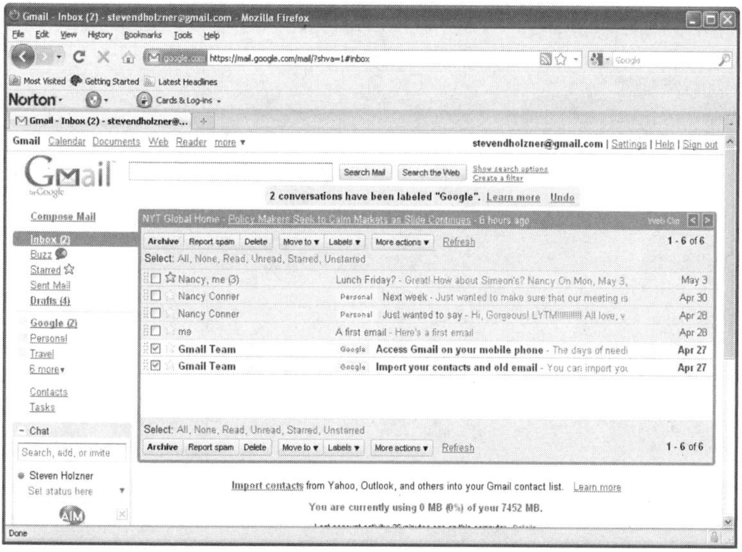

FIGURE 6.2 Adding a new label.

4. To return to the Inbox, click the **Inbox** link at the left in the page.

There's another way to create a new label as well—here's how:

1. Click the **Settings** link. Gmail opens the Settings page.

2. Click the **Labels** tab. This opens the Labels settings page, as shown in Figure 6.3.

3. To create a new label, enter the text of the label in **Create a New Label**, and click **Create**.

4. To return to the Inbox, click the **Inbox** link at the left in the page.

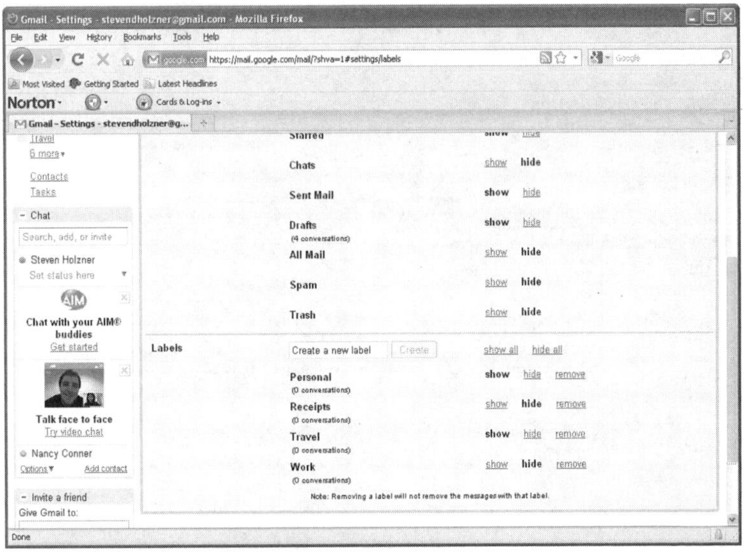

FIGURE 6.3   The labels settings page.

Sorting Mail by Labels

When you've labeled messages, you can sort those messages using those labels. For example, if you've given eight messages a particular label, you can click that label in the list of links at the left in any Gmail page and instantly see only those emails with that label.

Here's how to sort by label:

1. Click the label you want to sort by in the left pane of links. For example, clicking the **Google** link created in the previous task displays only emails that have been tagged with that link, as shown in Figure 6.4.

2. To return to the Inbox, click the **Inbox** link.

That's all you need to do to sort your mail by label.

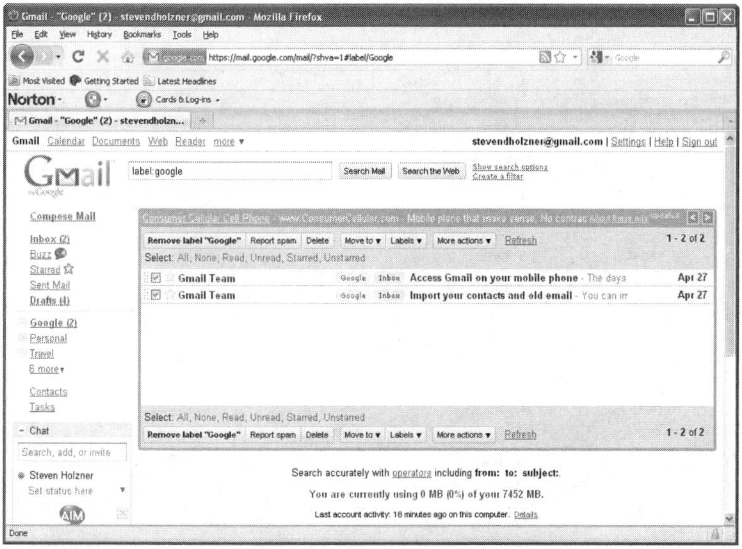

FIGURE 6.4 Sorting messages by label.

Editing Labels

You can also edit labels, changing their text. To edit a label name, follow these steps:

1. Click the down arrow that appears when you hover the mouse pointer over the label you want to edit. Gmail opens a drop-down menu.

2. Select the **Rename** item in the drop-down menu. Gmail will display the dialog box you see in Figure 6.5.

3. Edit the label name.

4. Click the **OK** button.

As you can see, renaming a label is simple.

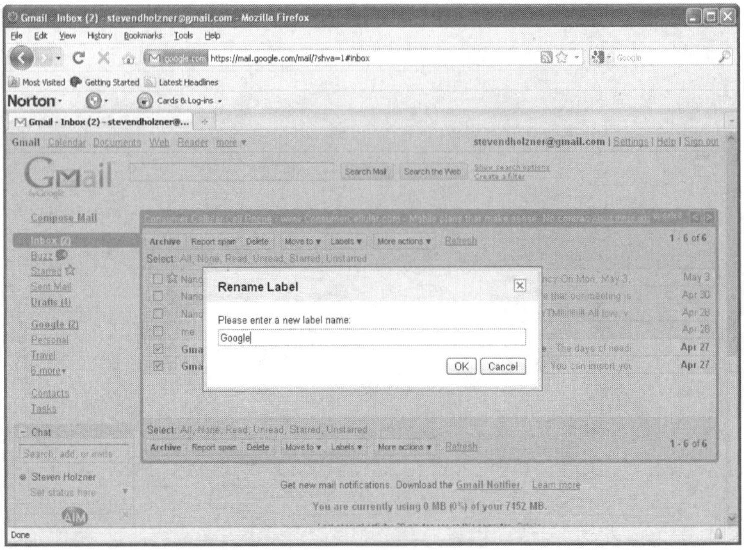

FIGURE 6.5   Editing a label.

Organizing Labels

You can also control which labels appear in your list on the left. To show or hide labels, do this:

1. Click the **Settings** link. Gmail opens the Settings page.

2. Click the **Labels** tab. Gmail displays the Labels Settings page, as shown in Figure 6.6.

3. Click the **Show** or **Hide** link, as you want, next to each label to show or hide that label.

4. To return to the Inbox, click the **Inbox** link.

If you have labels you rarely use anymore, consider hiding them to keep your other labels more accessible.

> TIP: **Showing/Hiding Labels**
>
> You can also show or hide one label at a time by clicking the down arrow to the left of each label and selecting the correct menu item.

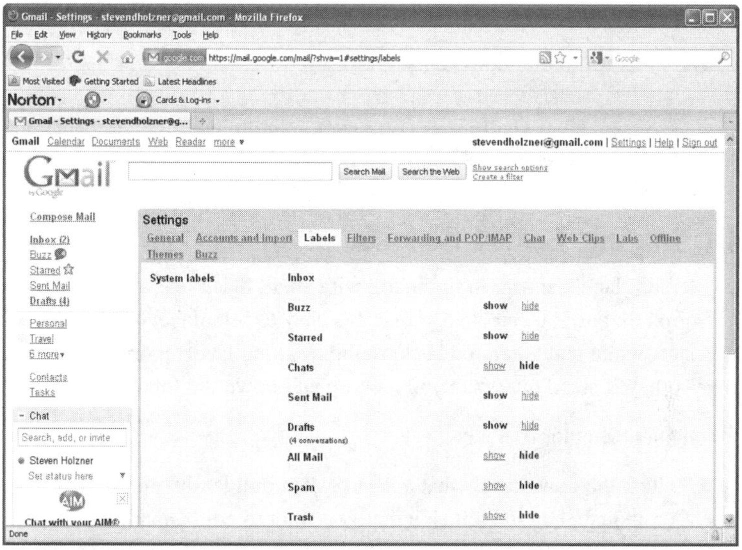

FIGURE 6.6   Showing or hiding labels.

Deleting Labels

You can delete labels as well, but you can delete only these labels:

▶ Personal

▶ Receipts

▶ Travel

▶ Work

You can delete the above labels or labels that you've created. Want to delete a label? Follow these steps:

1. Click the **Settings** link. Gmail opens the Settings page.

2. Click the **Labels** tab. Gmail displays the Labels Settings page.

3. Click the **Remove** link, as you want, next to each label to remove that label.

4. Click **OK** in the confirming dialog box that opens.

5. To return to the Inbox, click the **Inbox** link.

If you've got a label you're sure you're not going to use anymore, deleting it can get it out of your hair.

Changing Label Colors

By default, labels appear in the Inbox with small black text and a white background, but you can change that. It's easy to set a label to have, for instance, white text and a red background. Making labels more dramatic means they'll stand out when you look up and down the Inbox.

To change the color of a label:

1. Click the down arrow that appears when you let the mouse rest on the label on the left side that you want to edit. Gmail opens a drop-down menu, as shown in Figure 6.7.

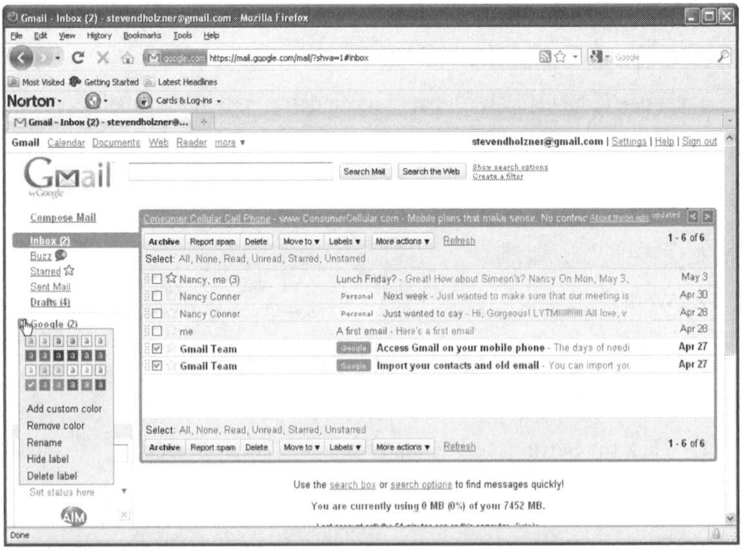

FIGURE 6.7 Changing a label's color scheme.

2. Select the new color and background from the palette in the drop-down menu.

Gmail displays the label's new color scheme immediately in the Inbox.

That's it—you've changed the color scheme of a label.

Searching Using Labels

What if you wanted to search only your mail tagged with a specific label—could you do it?

Yes—in fact, there is more than one way to do so. Here's what to do:

1. Click the **Show Search Options** link at the top of the page. Gmail opens the Search Options box.

2. Enter the information pinpointing what you'd like to search for. The possibilities are as follows:

   ▶ From—Search for mail from a specific person.

   ▶ To—Search for mail to a specific person.

   ▶ Subject—Search for mail with a particular subject.

   ▶ Has the Words—Lets you search the body of mail for specific words.

   ▶ Doesn't Have—Lets you search for mail that doesn't have specific words.

   ▶ Has Attachment—Check this check box if you want to search only mail that has an attachment.

   ▶ Date Within—Search mail with the date within a specified range of the date you enter. The possible ranges are the following:

      ▶ 1 day

      ▶ 3 days

      ▶ 1 week

▶ 2 weeks

▶ 1 month

▶ 2 months

▶ 6 months

▶ 1 year

3. Click the **Search** drop-down list. This opens a list that allows you to specify where to search.

4. Select the label from the drop-down list that tags mail you want to search.

5. Click the **Search Mail** button.

Gmail searches your mail and displays the results.

There's another way to search your mail using labels:

1. Enter your search term into the search box.

2. Add your search criteria to the search box. To specify a label, enter **label:** followed by the label's text.

For example, to search only mail from Edward with the label Friends, enter this in addition to the search term in the search box: **from:Edward label:Friends**.

If a label has a space in its name, such as My employees, hyphenate the label's name like this: **label:My-employees**.

3. Click the **Search Mail** button. Gmail displays the messages that match your criteria.

Moving Mail Between Labels

Want to move a message to a new label? No problem. Suppose, for exam-ple, that your former friend Tina didn't accept your dinner party invitation. You can move mail from Tina from Friends to the Enemies label (assum-ing you have an Enemies label). Here's how to move mail between labels:

1. Check the check box(es) to the left of the mail message(s) you want to move to a new label.

2. Click the **Move To** button. Gmail will display a drop-down list of labels that you can move the currently-selected message(s) to.

3. Select the new label from the drop-down list. Gmail applies the new label to the message(s).

That's it—now you can change labels in a message at any time.

Adding Multiple Labels to a Message

Gmail lets you apply multiple labels to the same message. Just follow these steps:

1. Check the check box(es) to the left of the mail message(s) you want to apply multiple labels to.

2. Click the **Labels** button. Gmail will display a drop-down list of labels.

3. Select a label from the drop-down list and click **Apply**. Gmail applies the new label to the message(s).

4. Repeat steps 3 and 4 for other labels you want to apply to the message(s).

You can see a sample message in the Inbox with multiple labels in Figure 6.8.

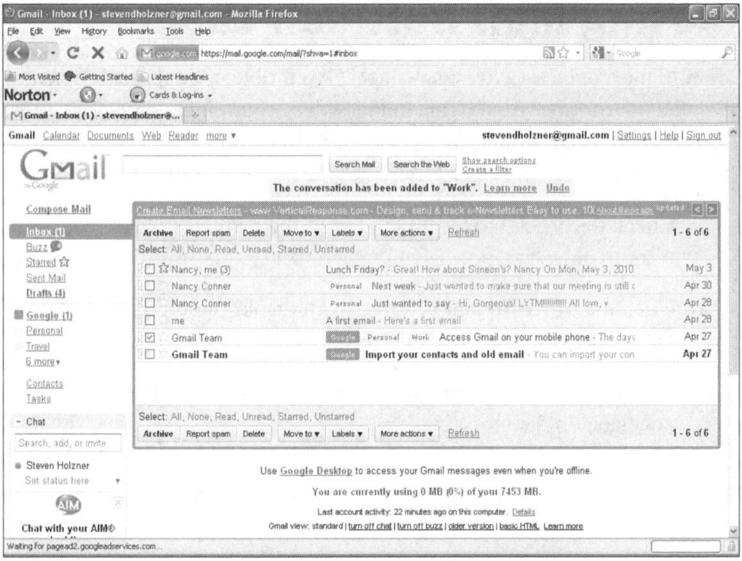

FIGURE 6.8   Adding multiple labels to one message.

Many messages can benefit from multiple labels, and now you can add them to those messages.

Using Tasks

Gmail tasks are to-do items in a list. For example, you might want to remind yourself to purchase cookies and have lunch with Nancy—no problem if you're using a task list.

To see your current tasks, just click the **Tasks** link at the left in any Gmail page. That opens the Tasks list at right, as shown in Figure 6.9.

Each task is prefaced with a check box that you can check to indicate you've taken care of that task.

When you click the **Pop-out** button (the upward arrow at the upper right in the Tasks list), the Tasks window opens as its own window, as shown in Figure 6.10. (We'll use the Tasks list in pop-out mode for clarity throughout the rest of this lesson.) To pop the Tasks list back into the Gmail page, click the **Pop-in** button—a downward-pointing arrow at the upper left in the Tasks window.

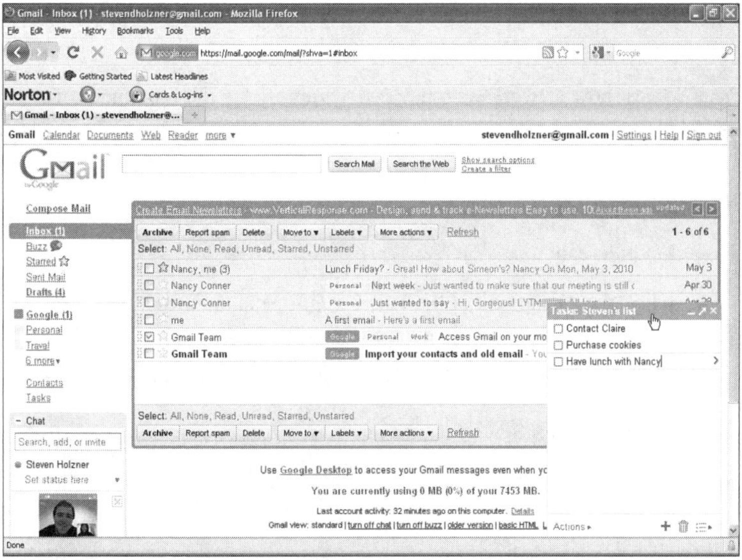

FIGURE 6.9   The Tasks list.

FIGURE 6.10   The Tasks list popped out.

To close the Tasks list, click the **X** box at the upper right or press the Esc key.

You'll learn how to work with the Tasks window for the remainder of this lesson.

Creating a Task

How do you create a task? It's easy:

1. Click the **Tasks** link at the left. Gmail opens the Tasks list.

2. Click the Tasks list. This will cause a blinking cursor to appear in the list.

3. Type your task as you would into a word processor. This adds the task to the list (Gmail adds a check box to the front of the task automatically).

To create an additional task, press Enter; Gmail skips to the next line, displays a check box and gives you a blinking cursor to enter the new task (alternatively, you can click the + button at the bottom of the Tasks list to create a new task).

You can also create a task from a Gmail message. In that case, Gmail will add the subject of the message as a new task and add a link to the task to the actual mail message. Here's how to create task from a mail message:

1. In the Inbox, check the check box to the left of the message you want to create a task from.

2. Click the **More Actions** drop-down menu and select **Add to Tasks**. This will cause Gmail to add the new task to the list.

   You can see an example at the top of Figure 6.11, where the subject of the mail message was Lunch Friday?

> TIP: **Adding New Tasks to the Middle of a List**
> You can also add new tasks to the middle of a list by clicking the beginning or end of an existing task and pressing Enter.

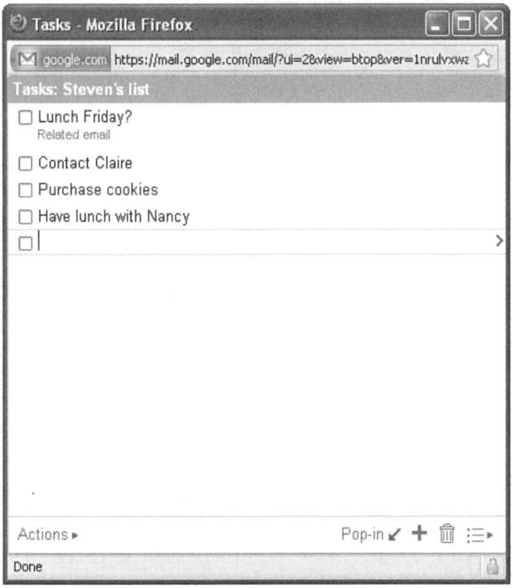

FIGURE 6.11   A task created from a mail message.

Create Subtasks

In addition to tasks, you can also create subtasks, which appear indented under tasks, as shown in Figure 6.12.

You can create subtasks easily using the Tasks list. Here's how:

1. Click the **Tasks** link. Gmail opens the Tasks list.

2. Click the **Tasks** list. This will cause a blinking cursor to appear in the list.

3. Press the Tab key. This causes Gmail to indent the current task, including its check box.

4. Type your subtask as you would into a word processor. This adds the subtask to the list.

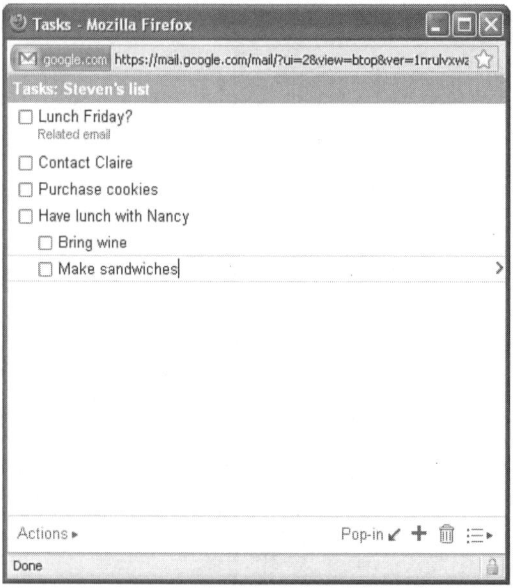

FIGURE 6.12   Two indented subtasks.

> NOTE: **Indenting Tasks**
>
> Note that when you press Tab, all the following tasks you enter are indented. To undo the indention, press Shift+Tab.

Checking Off Tasks

When you're done with a task, you can check off the task. And you can hide checked-off tasks to get them out of the way. To do so, follow these steps:

1. Click the **Tasks** link. Gmail opens the Tasks list.

2. Check the check box next to any task you want to check off. You can see an example in Figure 6.13. Note that checking off a task will automatically check off any subtasks, as shown in the figure.

3. To hide the checked tasks, select the **Clear Completed Tasks** item in the **Actions** drop-down list. This causes Gmail to hide all checked tasks.

FIGURE 6.13   A checked-off task.

TIP: **Viewing Hidden Completed Tasks**

Want to view your now-hidden completed tasks? Select the **View Completed Tasks** item from the **Actions** drop-down list.

Moving a Task

You might have arranged your tasks in some order and now want to move a task up or down the list. That's easy—just follow these steps:

1. From the Inbox click the **Tasks** link. Gmail opens the Tasks list.

2. To move a task, position the mouse cursor to the left of the task's check box, press the left mouse button, and drag the task to its new position in the list. You can see an example in Figure 6.14 where two tasks have been exchanged.

Moving tasks up and down lets you reprioritize your tasks.

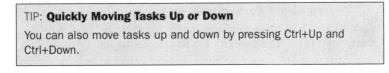

FIGURE 6.14   Moving a task within a list.

TIP: **Quickly Moving Tasks Up or Down**
You can also move tasks up and down by pressing Ctrl+Up and Ctrl+Down.

Printing Tasks

Have you just typed up your grocery list into the Tasks list and want to print it out to take to the store? Just follow these steps:

1. From the Inbox, click the **Tasks** link. Gmail opens the Tasks list.

2. Select **Print Task List** in the **Actions** drop-down menu. A Print dialog box appears.

3. Click **Print** in the Print dialog box.

That's all it takes.

LESSON 7

Getting Some Buzz in Gmail

In this lesson, you'll learn how to use Google Buzz, the built-in social networking application that comes with Gmail.

Google Buzz is a mini-messaging system not unlike Twitter, and it has become very popular. Because Buzz is built right in to Gmail, we're going to take a look at it in this lesson and the next.

How does it work? With Buzz, you can enter some text such as "It's snowing here. Rats!" or "We won the big game!" and other people will see what you've posted.

When people watch what you've posted, they're called your *followers*. So when someone follows you, he'll be shown what you've posted automatically.

When you watch what someone else posts, you're following him.

Thus, Buzz becomes a game of following and being followed. You have to sign up to follow a particular person, and other people have to sign up to follow you (you can't sign up to have your own followers). You'll see how that process works here and in the next lesson.

Buzz is all about short conversations. What you post appears in the Buzz window of people following you, and the posts of people you're following show up in your Buzz window. It's a great way to keep in touch.

NOTE: **More About Google Buzz**

Want to learn more about Google Buzz? See my companion book *Sams Teach Yourself Google Buzz* to get all the details.

When you've signed up for Gmail, you've already signed up for Buzz, so let's get started.

Starting the Buzz

Because you already have a Gmail account, you already have a Buzz account. To get started with Buzz, do this:

1. From the Inbox click the **Buzz** link at the left. This opens the page you see in Figure 7.1.

FIGURE 7.1   The Buzz video.

If you want to, watch the Buzz video.

2. Click the **Get Started with Buzz** button. Gmail displays the page you see in Figure 7.2.

And you're now in Buzz. Not much is happening here, however. Take a look at the next task to see how to start following people.

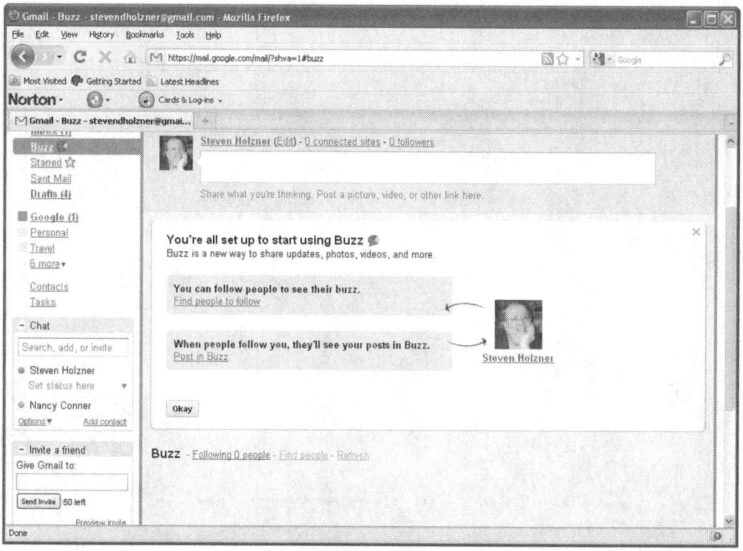

FIGURE 7.2   Getting started with Buzz.

Following People in Buzz

In the previous task, we got started with Buzz and ended up with a page that displayed a Find People to Follow link. In this task, we're going to follow that link and start following people on Buzz.

1. In the opening Buzz page (shown in Figure 7.2), click the **Find People to Follow** link. Gmail displays the page you see in Figure 7.3.

2. To find people to follow, enter the name or email address of a Gmail user into the text box and click the **Search** button.

You'll see matches displayed in the page, as shown in Figure 7.4.

3. Click the **Follow** link next to the people you want to follow.

4. Click the **Done** button.

If the people you're following have posted to Buzz recently, their posts will appear in your Buzz window at the bottom, as shown in Figure 7.5.

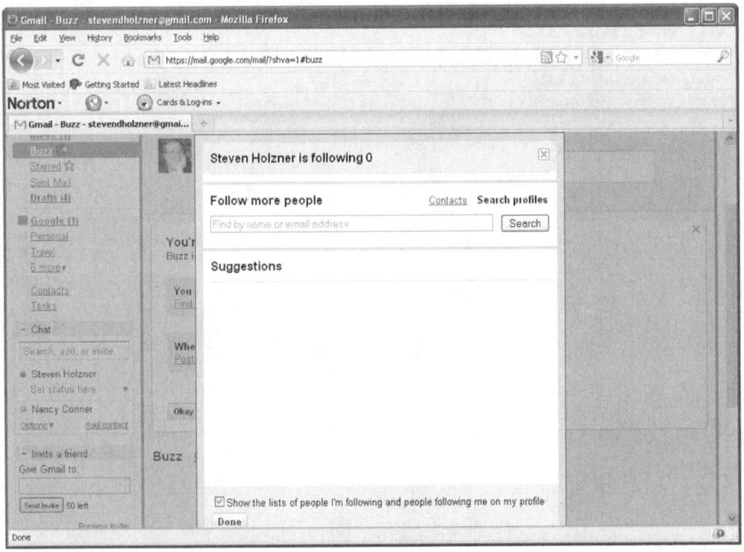

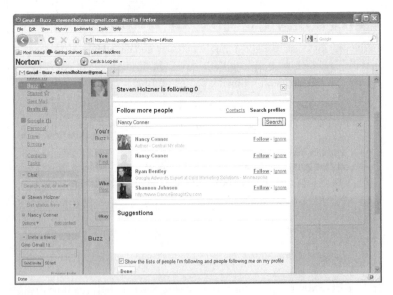

FIGURE 7.3 Finding people to follow.

FIGURE 7.4 Matches of Gmail users.

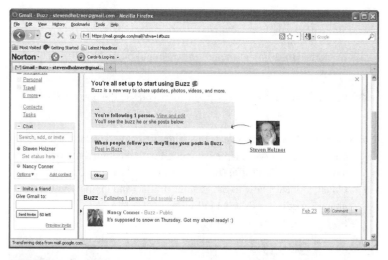

FIGURE 7.5 Reading some buzz.

Reading Some Buzz

If you want to read the buzz from the people you're following, just follow these steps:

1. Click the **Buzz** link at the left in the Gmail page. The Buzz page opens.

2. Scroll down in the Buzz window until your new buzz appears.

That's all it takes! To read your buzz, open the Buzz window and scroll down to see what's going on.

Commenting on Buzz

You can keep Buzz conversations going by commenting on posts. When you comment on a post, you add your own voice to that post, and everyone who saw the original post can see your comments. To comment on a buzz post, follow these steps:

1. Click the **Buzz** link at the left in the Gmail page. The Buzz page opens.

2. Scroll down in the Buzz window until you see the post you want to comment on.

3. Click the **Comment** link. If this is the first time you've posted a comment, Buzz will display a dialog box indicating that you have a default Google Profile (refer to Lesson 2, "Signing Up for Gmail," to learn how to create your profile) and giving you the chance to edit it, as shown in Figure 7.6.

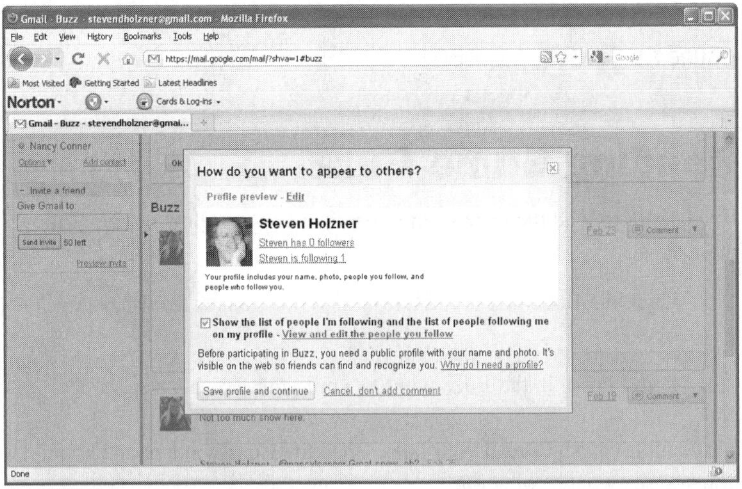

FIGURE 7.6   The first-time posting dialog box.

4. Click the **Save Profile and Continue** button to accept the default profile (or click the **Edit** link to edit your profile if you prefer to make changes to your profile). A text box opens for your comment, as shown in Figure 7.7.

5. Enter your comment in the text box.

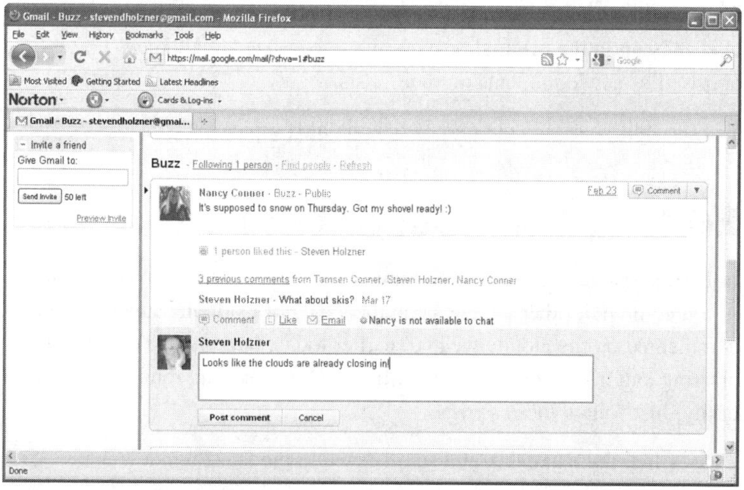

FIGURE 7.7 Entering a comment.

6. Click the **Post Comment** button. Buzz adds your comment to the current post, as shown in Figure 7.8.

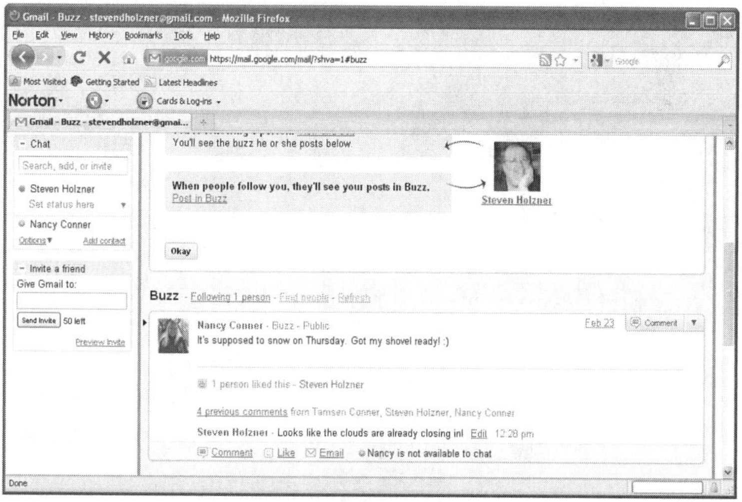

FIGURE 7.8 A new comment.

Commenting on posts like this keeps Buzz going. In fact, your comment
also ends up in the original poster's Inbox because Gmail keeps posters
apprised of new comments on their posts.

Want to edit your own comment? See the next topic.

Editing Your Comments

In Buzz, you can edit your own comments (on occasion, it would be nice
if you could edit other people's comments!). For example, suppose you
commented on the cloudy weather earlier today, but now the clouds are
clearing and it's becoming a beautiful day. You can edit your comment
easily. Just follow these steps:

1. Click the **Buzz** link and scroll down in the Buzz window until
you see the post you want to edit the comment in.

2. Click the **Edit** link following the comment. This link will appear
only for your own comments.

Buzz opens your comment in a text box, as shown in Figure 7.9.

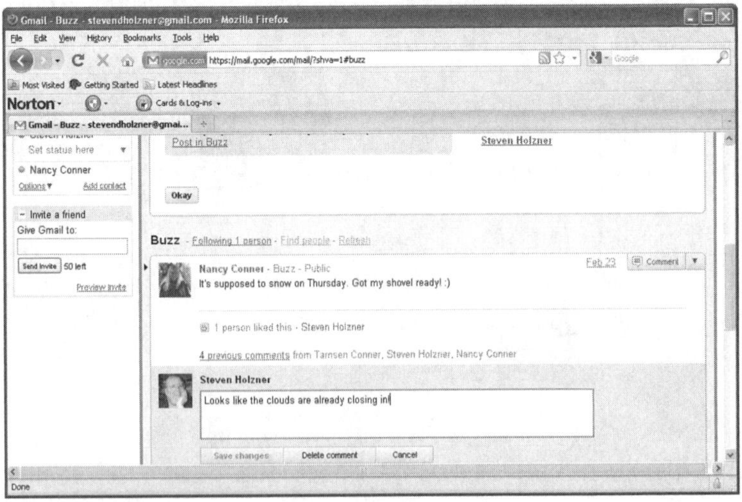

FIGURE 7.9   Editing a comment.

3. Edit your comment.

4. Click the **Save Changes** button. Buzz posts the new text of your comment, as shown in Figure 7.10.

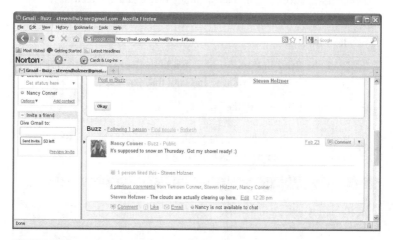

FIGURE 7.10   A newly edited comment.

It's that simple to edit your own comments.

Deleting Your Comments

What if you want to delete a comment entirely? Can you do that?

Yes, you can; follow these steps:

1. Click the **Buzz** link and scroll down in the Buzz window until you see the post you want to delete the comment from.

2. Click the **Edit** link following the comment. This link will appear only for your own comments.

Buzz opens your comment in a text box.

3. Click the **Delete Comment** button. Buzz removes the comment.

Deleting comments can be very useful at times, especially when you posted a comment in error.

Liking Posts

You can also use another option for commenting on the posts you read–you can "like" a post, which adds a smiley face and a comment that you liked the post.

Here's how to "like" a post:

1. Click the **Buzz** link and scroll down in the Buzz window until you see the post you want to indicate that you like.

2. Click the **Like** link in the post.

   Buzz adds the text "*n* people liked this", where *n* is a number, followed by your name, as shown in Figure 7.11.

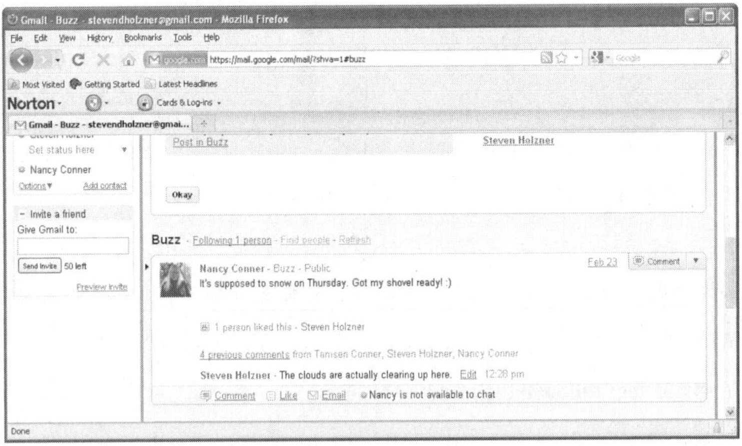

FIGURE 7.11   "Liking" a post.

Being able to "like" a post gives you the ability to give positive feedback to a post with a click.

> TIP: **Unliking a Post**
>
> After you've "liked" a post, the Like link doesn't go away, it just becomes "Un-like". Clicking the **Unlike** link remove the "like" you've added to the post. There's no way to add a frowning face icon to a

post to "un-like" it specifically. Google seems to be operating on the idea that if you don't have anything nice to say, don't say anything at all.

Emailing Posts

Is there a post you like so much you want other people to see it? You can email posts using—what else?—Gmail.

Here's how:

1. Click the **Buzz** link and scroll down in the Buzz window until you see the post you want to email.

2. Click the down arrow next to the **Comment** button.

Buzz opens a drop-down menu.

3. Select the **Email This Post** menu item (alternatively, you can click the Email link at the bottom of a post). Buzz opens the post for emailing using Gmail, of course, as shown in the window in Figure 7.12.

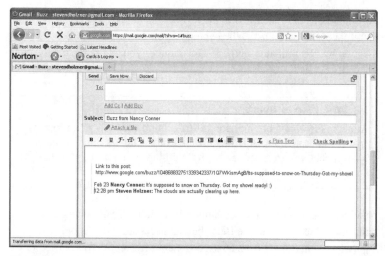

FIGURE 7.12 Emailing a Buzz post.

4. Enter the email address you want to send the post to in the **To** box. If you want to send the post to multiple email addresses, separate them with commas.

5. Edit the subject of the email in the **Subject** box if you want to.

6. Add any text to the email body itself that you want to.

7. Click the **Send** button to send the email.

That's all it takes to mail a post to someone.

Using Buzz with Mobile Phones

Google has set things up so you can use Buzz on your mobile phone, and it's just like using Buzz on a computer, except that you can also tag your post with your location. That's nice but, as some people point out, it can also pose a security risk because you're advertising that you're not home.

To read your Buzz with your mobile phone, go to buzz.google.com on your phone's browser. To read your buzz, click the **Following** link to see buzz from your friends.

To post some buzz, enter text in the text box that appears at the top of any Buzz page and click **Post**. When you post your buzz, you can geo-tag your location by accepting the suggested location, or you can refine the location yourself.

TIP: **Who Else Is Nearby?**
Want to see who's been posting Buzz around you? Click the **Nearby** link at the top of any Buzz page to see buzz that was posted nearby. You click the Buzz labels on the map that appears to read the actual buzz.

Note that not all mobile phones support Buzz fully. If your phone has a built-in browser, you can use Buzz, but not necessarily the Google Buzz app (which you can get from buzz.google.com web app). You can see various features and how well they're supported on various phones in Table 7.1.

TABLE 7.1   Support for Buzz by Mobile Phone Type

Feature	Android 2.0+	iPhone	BlackBerry	Nokia S60	Windows Mobile	Palm webOS
Buzz App (buzz.google.com web app)	Yes	Yes	Coming soon	Coming soon	Coming soon	Coming soon
Buzz Layer on Google Maps for mobile	Yes	Yes	Coming soon	Yes	Yes	
Buzz on a Place Page	Yes	Yes				
Voice shortcuts	Yes	Yes				
Buzz icon shortcuts	Yes	Yes				

Reading Every Post from a Particular Person

Suppose you've met someone interesting and want to read all posts by that person on Buzz. How can you do that? Follow these steps:

1. Click the **Buzz** link and scroll down in the Buzz window until you see a post by the person whose posts you want to see.

2. Click the name of the person at the beginning of the post.

The name is actually a link to the person's posts. Buzz opens a window listing all posts by that person, as shown in Figure 7.13.

Or you can also follow these steps to see all of someone's buzz:

1. Click the **Buzz** link and scroll down in the Buzz window until you see a post by the person whose posts you want to see.

2. Click the down arrow next to the **Comment** button.

   Buzz opens a drop-down menu.

3. Select the **View All Buzz From *xxxx***, where *xxxx* is the poster's name menu item.

   Buzz opens a window listing all posts from *xxxx*.

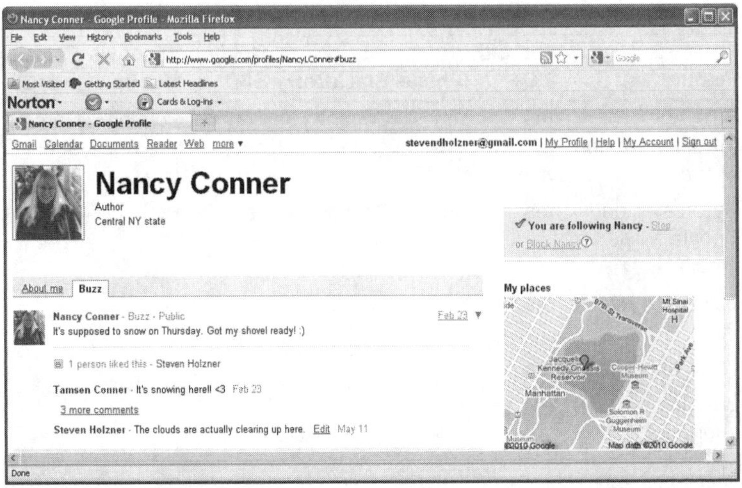

FIGURE 7.13   Reading all posts from a particular person.

This provides an easy way to let you catch up on all that a person has been posting.

Searching Buzz

This being Google, it would be very surprising if you couldn't search Buzz for specific keywords. In fact, you can search all Buzz and see who has been buzzing about topics of interest to you and start following those people if you want.

Just follow these steps:

1. Click the **Buzz** link at the left in the Gmail page. The Buzz page opens.

   Note that the button at the top of the page that originally read Search Mail now reads Search Buzz.

2. Enter the word or phrase you want to search your buzz for in the search box at the top of the page.

3. Click the **Search Buzz** button.

A list of posts that have matches to your search appears, as in Figure 7.14.

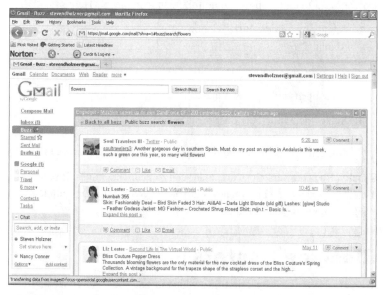

FIGURE 7.14 Searching Buzz.

TIP: **Following Someone Found in a Search**
If you want to follow someone you've found through a search, click the person's name in the beginning of the post, and then click the blue **Follow x** (with x being the person's name) button.

Muting Buzz Posts

On occasion, Buzz conversations might take turns that you're just not interested in. You might be an opera fan, for example, and be following a conversation that suddenly starts discussing the Opera browser.

How do you turn off a conversation? You can mute it. Muting a post stops any follow-ups from appearing in your Buzz stream. In addition, if you had commented on a post, all further comments on the post will also appear in your Inbox, unless you mute the post. When you mute a post, follow-ups do not appear in your Inbox.

Do you want to mute a post and all follow-up comments? Here's how:

1. Scroll down in the Buzz window until you see the post you want to mute.

2. Click the down arrow next to the Comment button.

   Buzz opens a drop-down menu.

3. Select the **Mute This Post** menu item.

   Buzz mutes the post, and it disappears from your Buzz window.

Usually, Buzz conversations are under control, but sometimes, it seems a topic just tickles someone's fancy and you get comment after comment. It's good to know you can mute such posts.

Blocking Posters

You can also block people on Buzz, which means you'll never see anything they post, including comments. If you want to block someone, follow these steps:

1. Scroll down in the Buzz window until you see a post from someone you want to block or containing a comment by someone you want to block.

2. Click the name of the person you want to block. Buzz opens that person's profile, as you see in Figure 7.15.

3. Click the **Block xxxx** link, where *xxxx* is the first name of the person you want to block.

4. Click the Yes button in the dialog box that opens.

   Buzz blocks the person for you. (You can see the **Block Nancy** link above the map in Figure 7.15.)

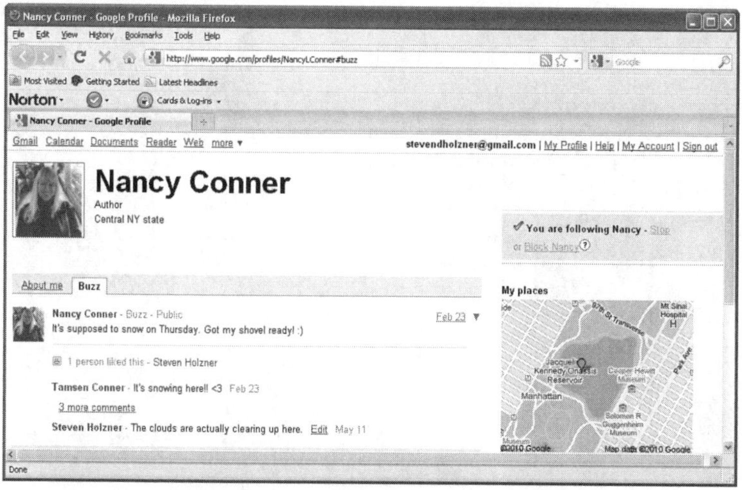

FIGURE 7.15   A person's Google Profile.

TIP: **Unblocking Someone**

Want to unblock someone? Follow the previous directions, and when you get to their profile page, you'll see the link has been changed to **Unblock**. Then click that link.

Seeing Who You're Following

It's not hard to get a list of the people you're following. Just do this:

1. Click your name at the top of the Buzz window. Buzz opens a new window showing your following information.

2. To see who you're following, click the ***xxxx* Is Following *n*** link, where *xxxx* is your name and *n* is a number. Buzz opens an information dialog, as you can see in Figure 7.16.

3. To see who is following you, click the ***xxxx* Has *n* Followers** link, where *xxxx* is your name and *n* is a number.

Want to find more people to follow? Take a look at the next task.

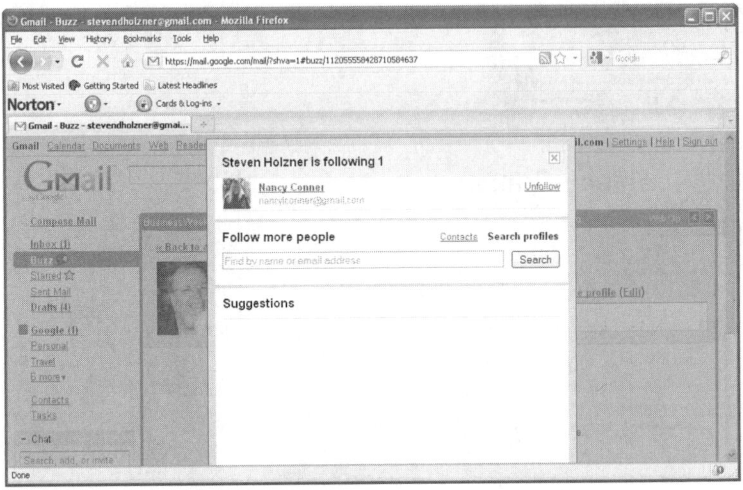

FIGURE 7.16   The Following info window.

Finding More People to Follow

You can find people to follow easily from your contacts or by searching Google profiles. Here's how:

1. Click your name at the top of the Buzz window. Buzz opens a new window showing your following information.

2. Click the ***xxxx* Is Following *n*** link, where *xxxx* is your name and *n* is a number. Buzz opens an information dialog.

3. Enter the word or phrase you want to search for in the Follow More People box and click the **Search** button. Buzz displays a list of matches.

4. To follow one of the people in the search results, click the **Follow** link next to that person's entry in the list of matches.

5. Click the **Done** button to close the dialog box.

That's it—now the people you've selected are added to the list of people you're following.

"Unfollowing" People

Following too many people? Need to "unfollow" a few? Use these steps to stop following someone using a post:

1. Scroll down in the Buzz window until you see a post by the person whose posts you want to stop following.

2. Click the down arrow next to the **Comment** button.

Buzz opens a drop-down menu.

3. Select the **Stop Following** *xxxx,* where *xxxx* is the poster's name menu item.

Buzz removes that person from the list of people you're following.

You don't need to see a post from someone to stop following them. You can also "unfollow" people this way:

1. Click your name at the top of the Buzz window. Buzz opens a new window showing your Following information.

2. To get the list of who you're following, click the *xxxx* **Is Following** *n* link, where *xxxx* is your name and *n* is a number. Buzz opens an information dialog.

3. To "unfollow" a person, click the **Unfollow** link next to the person's name.

Reporting Abuse

Need to report something you've read as abusive? Here's how you do it:

1. Scroll down in the Buzz window until you see the post you want to report.

2. Click the down arrow next to the **Comment** button in the post.

Buzz opens a drop-down menu.

3. Select the **Report Abuse** menu item.

4. Select the correct radio button in the dialog box that opens; then click the Submit button.

Buzz reports the post, and it disappears from your Buzz window.

If you're in doubt about abuse, it's best to report it.

LESSON 8

Posting Your Buzz

In this lesson, you'll learn all about how to post some Buzz. After all, that's what Buzz is all about—posting your thoughts so others can see them.

All About Posting Buzz

We're going to post some Buzz and see all the options here, such as making posts private, posting links, photos, and videos—even posting via email.

If you can post it to Buzz, you'll find it here in this lesson. Communicating with others in Buzz starts with posting your buzz, so let's get started.

Writing Some Buzz

Got some Buzz you want to post? Cat doing funny tricks? Floodwaters beginning to rise? Just follow these steps to post some Buzz:

1. From the Inbox click the **Buzz** link. The Buzz page appears.

2. Click the top text box in the Buzz window (this text box has the caption **Share What You're Thinking. Post a Picture, Video, or Other Link Here**). Clicking this box normally adds a blinking cursor to the box, but if this is the first time you've posted (including any comments on other posts), you'll see a dialog box that asks you to create a profile if you haven't already done so.

3. Click the **Save Profile and Continue** button to accept the default profile if Buzz displays the profile dialog box (or click the **Edit** link to edit your profile if you choose). The Buzz window reappears, this time with a larger text box for you to enter your post in, as shown in Figure 8.1.

4. Enter the text of your post in the large text box.

5. Click the **Post** button. By default, your post is public, which means it goes to your profile and to all your followers.

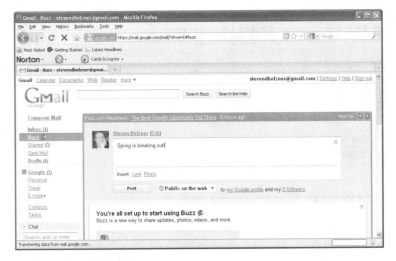

FIGURE 8.1   Creating a first post.

Your new buzz also appears at the bottom of your Buzz window, as shown in Figure 8.2.

And that's it—it was easy. Now you can post on Buzz.

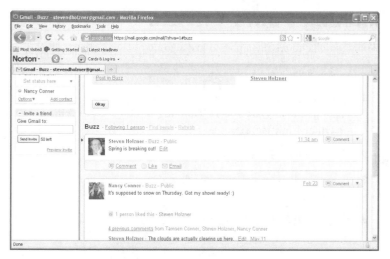

FIGURE 8.2   A new Buzz post.

Making Posts Public

Buzz lets you post either publicly or privately. Public posts can be seen by your followers and also on your Google profile. Private posts can be seen only by the contacts you specify.

By default, all posts you make are public, but you can ensure a post is public by following these steps:

1. Click the top text box in the Buzz window (this text box has the caption **Share What You're Thinking. Post a Picture, Video, or Other Link Here**).

2. Enter the text of your post.

3. Select the **Public on the Web** option in the drop-down list box next to the Post button. Note that this is the default option.

4. Click the **Post** button to post your message.

How do you make a post private? See the next task.

Making Posts Private

Would you like to restrict a post to just a group of Gmail contacts?

Follow these steps:

1. Click the top text box in the Buzz window (this text box has the caption **Share What You're Thinking. Post a Picture, Video, or Other Link Here**).

2. Enter the text of your post.

3. Select the **Private** option in the drop-down list box next to the Post button.

4. Click the **Post to a Group** link that appears. This causes Buzz to display your groups, as shown in Figure 8.3.

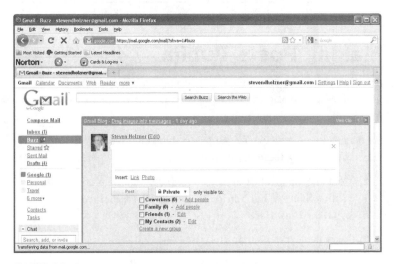

FIGURE 8.3   Posting to a group.

5. Check the group(s) you want to post to.

6. Click the **Post** button to post your message. Buzz posts to the groups you've selected.

As you can see, it's easy to post to multiple groups this way as well—just check multiple check boxes.

> NOTE: **Private Posts Appear with a Lock Icon**
>
> When you make your posts private, they appear with a small pad-lock icon appearing in the first line of the post to indicate that they are private posts.

Replying Privately to Posts (@ Replies)

What if you want to reply privately to a post? Can you do that? Yes, you can send a response to a post directly to the poster's Inbox. And the reply won't appear in anyone's Buzz stream.

In other words, you can reply entirely privately to a Buzz post, and no one but the original poster will see your response.

Here's how to do it:

> NOTE: **Must Be a Gmail Contact**
>
> Note that to use this technique in Buzz, the poster of the message you're replying to must be in your Gmail contacts, and you must know that person's Gmail username.

Just follow these steps to reply privately to a post:

1. Scroll down in the Buzz window until you find the post that you want to reply privately to.

2. Click the **Comment** link in the post. Clicking this link makes a text box appear for your comment.

3. Begin your comment with @*username*, where *username* is the original poster's username. You can see an example in Figure 8.4.

   If you begin your comment with @*username*, Buzz will send your reply to the person's Inbox, not to any Buzz stream.

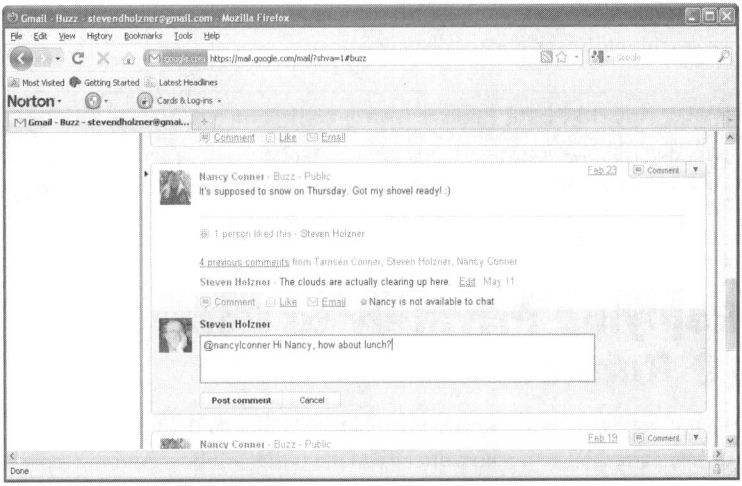

FIGURE 8.4   Replying privately to a post.

4. Click the **Post Comment** button. Buzz sends your comment to the original poster's Inbox.

Great! Now you can send private messages on Buzz.

Getting Buzzed in Your Inbox

Buzz posts are sent to your Gmail Inbox by default (you can change these in the Settings page) when people comment on your posts, when people comment on posts after you comment on them, or when people comment on posts after you've @replied on those posts.

Want to read your Buzz that's sent to your Inbox? Here's how:

1. Scroll up and down in the Inbox, if necessary, to find the Buzz message you want to read. Buzz messages in your Inbox have a subject line that starts with Buzz: followed with text from the original post, followed by the **Buzz** link, as you can see at the top of the Inbox in Figure 8.5.

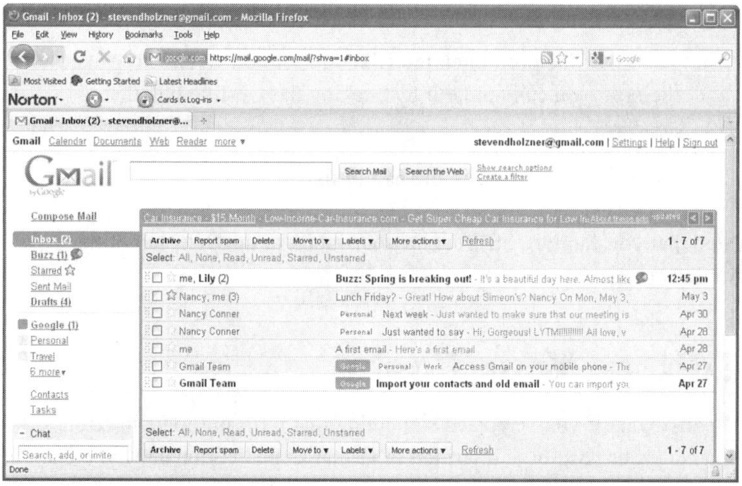

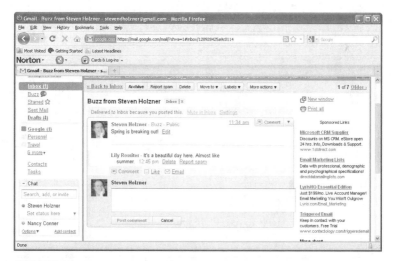

FIGURE 8.5 A Buzz post in your Inbox.

2. Click the subject of the Buzz post in your Inbox to open it. Clicking the subject opens the Buzz post in the center pane, as shown in Figure 8.6.

FIGURE 8.6 A Buzz post from your Inbox.

3. To comment on the post, click the **Comment** link.

4. To "Like" the post, click the **Like** link. If you've already "liked" the post, you can unlike it by clicking the **Un-like** link that appears.

5. To email the post, click the **Email** link.

Note that you can turn off Buzz in your Inbox in the Buzz tab of the Settings page.

Editing Your Posts

Uh oh—what if you've posted something that turns out to be in error? Can you edit your post, or is it written in virtual stone? Fortunately, you can edit your posts after you've made them. Here's how:

1. Scroll down in the Buzz window until you find your post that you want to edit.

2. Click the **Edit** link in the post. Clicking this link opens the post for editing, as you see in Figure 8.7.

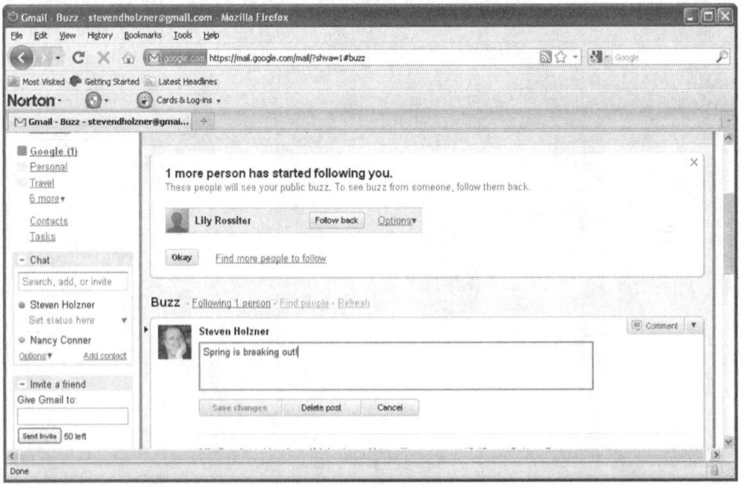

FIGURE 8.7   Editing your post.

3. Make your edits to the post.

4. Click the **Save Changes** button. Buzz saves the newly edited post, which is updated everywhere it appears in Buzz.

And that's it—now you can change your posts at any time.

Posting by Email

Want another way to post your buzz? You can post using email, as long as that email is Gmail. You can email your buzz to Buzz, as long as your return email address is the Gmail account you want the buzz to originate from.

Here's how to post buzz from email:

1. From the Inbox click the **Compose Mail** link. Gmail opens its Compose Mail window as shown in Figure 8.8.

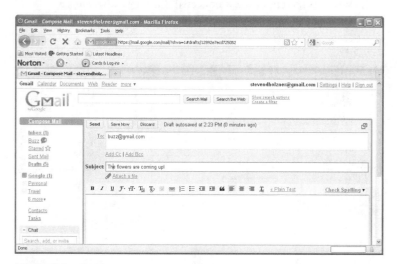

FIGURE 8.8   The Gmail mail composer window.

2. Enter **buzz@gmail.com** in the To box. Note that you have to mail the post to your Buzz posts from the Gmail account that is connected to the Buzz account you want the post to appear from.

3. Enter the buzz you want to post in the Subject box. Note that your post is taken from the Subject line alone. The body of the message is totally ignored.

4. If you want to attach files, such as photos or videos to include in your post, click the **Attach a File** link and follow the directions.

5. Click the **Send** button.

Note that all posts you make by email are public by default, but you can change that. See the next task.

Posting Privately by Email

If you want to post privately by email, it takes a few extra steps. Here's what to do

1. Within Buzz, click the *n* **Connected Sites** link, where *n* is a number. Clicking this link opens the dialog box you can see in Figure 8.9.

FIGURE 8.9   The Buzz Connected Sites dialog box.

2. Click the **Add** link next to the **Posted via buzz@gmail** link. Note that Buzz changes the Add link to a Public label and also adds an Edit link next to that label.

3. Click the **Edit** link. Doing so makes the drop-down list box you can see in Figure 8.10 appear.

FIGURE 8.10   Editing privacy settings.

4. Select **Private** in the drop-down list box. Buzz will show check boxes for all your Gmail groups.

5. Select the group(s) you want to post privately to.

6. Click the **Done** button.

7. Click the **Save** button.

That's all it takes—now what you post to Buzz via email will be posted privately.

Getting to Know Your Followers

Want to know more about who is following you? If they've posted or commented on Buzz, they'll have a Google profile, and you can take a look at that. Here's how:

1. Click the *n* **Followers** link, where *n* is a number (if *n* is 1, this will be **1 Follower**). Clicking this link opens a dialog box displaying your followers.

2. To see more about a follower, click that person's name. Clicking the name opens that person's Buzz posts in a posts window.

3. To see the person's Google profile, click the **Google Profile** link in the person's posts window. Clicking this link opens that Google Profile in a new window. There are two tabs in this window, About Me and Buzz (the Buzz tab will not appear if the person has specified they want to be private).

4. Click the **About Me** tab to see that person's full profile.

Note that if that person has accepted the default profile just so he or she can post on Buzz, there won't be much information in that profile.

Posting Links to Online Articles to Buzz

You might run across an article online that you want to post on Buzz. After all, if the article interests you, you can tell your friends. It's easy to post links to articles in Buzz—here's how:

1. Click the top text box in the Buzz window (this text box has the caption **Share What You're Thinking. Post a Picture, Video, or Other Link Here**).

2. Enter the text of your post.

3. Click the **Link** under the post. Buzz displays a text box for your link, as shown in Figure 8.11.

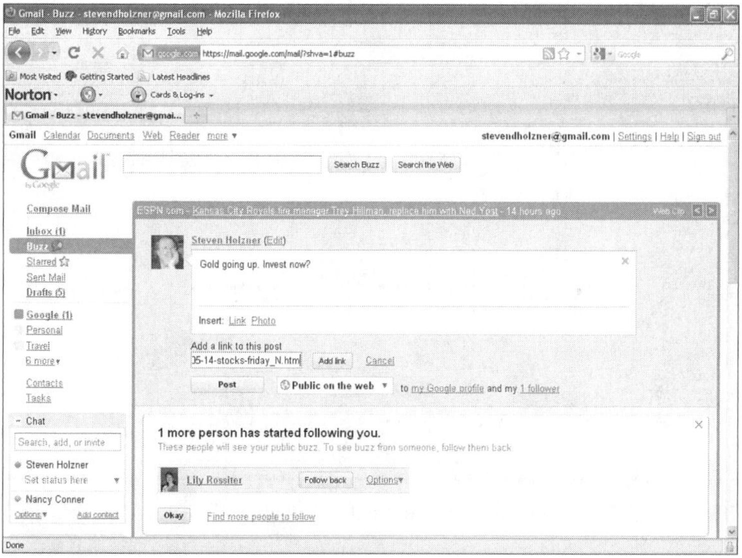

FIGURE 8.11 Posting a link.

4. Enter the URL of the link in this text box.

5. Click the **Add Link** button to add the link to your post. Buzz searches the article online.

6. If the article has images, Buzz gives you the chance to include them in your post. Click the images you want to include. An example is shown in Figure 8.12.

7. Click the **Post** button to send your post to Buzz.

Now you've posted a link. You can see an example in Figure 8.13; note that Buzz displays some text from the link as well as the photo you've selected.

FIGURE 8.12 Posting images with a link.

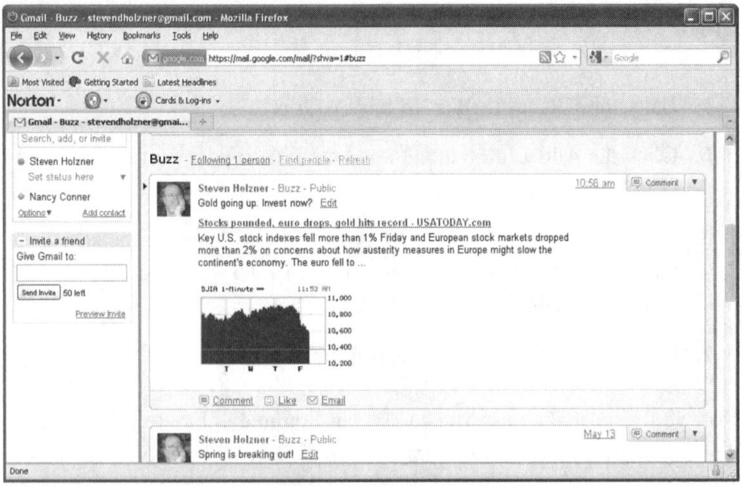

FIGURE 8.13 A post containing a link.

Posting Photos to Buzz

What if you want to post that photo of your sweetie from Waikiki beach?

No problem. Just follow these steps:

1. Click the top text box in the Buzz window (this text box has the caption **Share What You're Thinking. Post a Picture, Video, or Other Link Here**).

2. Enter the text of your post.

3. Click the **Photo** link under the post. Buzz displays a dialog box asking you to log in to your Google account. Your Gmail address is already entered as your username.

4. Enter your password and click the **Sign In** button. Buzz displays a dialog box with the caption **Add Photos to Post**.

5. Click the **Choose Photos to Upload** button. Buzz displays a dialog box that lets you browse to the photos you want to upload.

6. Browse to your photos and select them in the dialog box.

7. Click the **Open** button in the dialog box. Buzz displays the photo(s) you've selected.

8. Click the **Add Photos to Post** button. The photo or photos you've selected appear in your post, as shown in Figure 8.14.

9. Click the **Post** button to send your post to Buzz.

What does the post with your photo actually look like? You can see an example in Figure 8.15.

Note that the photo in Figure 8.15 is a thumbnail; clicking it takes you to the original photo.

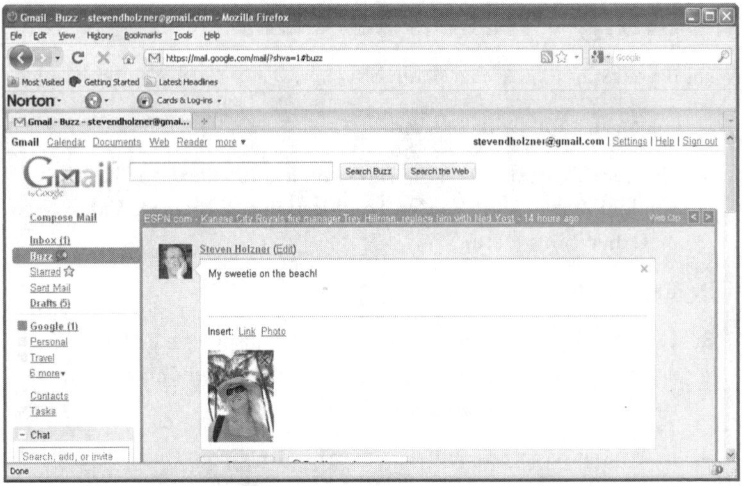

FIGURE 8.14   Preparing to post a photo.

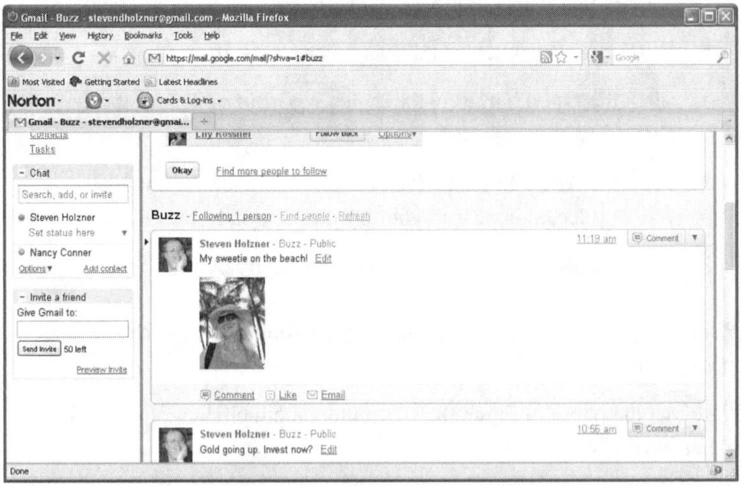

FIGURE 8.15   A post containing a photo.

Adding Captions to Your Photos

It's simple to add captions to your posted photos—here's how:

1. Click the link **Photo** under the post.

2. Click the **Choose Photos to Upload** button. Buzz displays a dialog box that lets you browse to the photos you want to upload.

3. Browse to your photo and select it in the dialog box.

4. Click the **Open** button in the dialog box. Buzz displays the photo(s) you've selected.

5. Select the photo you want to add a caption to by clicking it. The link **Add a Caption** appears under the photo.

6. Click the **Add a Caption** link. A text box appears for you to enter your caption in, as shown in Figure 8.16.

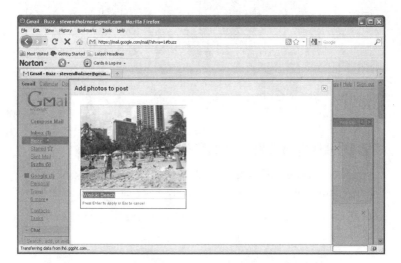

FIGURE 8.16   Adding a caption.

7. Enter your caption in the text box and press Enter. The new caption appears in the photo (not below or on top, but inside the photo).

8. Click the **Add Photos to Post** button. The photo appears in your post, as shown in Figure 8.17.

9. Click the **Post** button to send your post to Buzz.

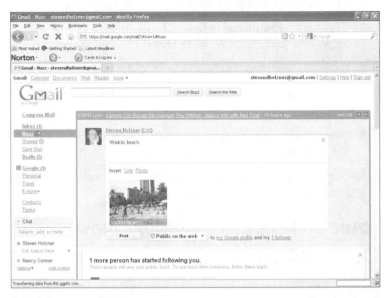

FIGURE 8.17   A photo with a caption.

Keeping Your Photos Private

You can restrict your photos to a certain group of your contacts in Buzz, if you like (those embarrassing beach photos!). Just follow these steps:

1. Browse to your photos and select them in the dialog box.

2. Click the **Open** button in the dialog box. Buzz displays the photo(s) you've selected.

3. Click the **Add Photos to Post** button. The photo or photos you've selected appear in your post.

4. Click the down arrow next to the **Public on the Web** list box item, and select the **Private** item. Buzz lists the group you most recently posted to. If you accept that group, skip to step 7.

5. Click the **Post to Other Groups** link. Buzz displays your groups with check boxes.

6. Check the check boxes corresponding to the groups you want to post to. If you want to create a new group, click the **Create a New Group** link.

7. Click the **Post** button to post to Buzz.

Keeping your photos private can be a good option.

Posting Videos to Buzz

What about posting videos on Buzz? Your options are a little limited because Buzz won't let you host videos directly. Instead, you can post a link to a video already hosted online and usually in Buzz; that means posting a link to a YouTube video (note that Google owns YouTube).

Want to post a YouTube video on Buzz? Follow these steps:

1. Enter the text of your post in Buzz.

2. Go to the YouTube page for the video you want to post to Buzz and copy the URL from the URL box in the YouTube page (example: http://www.youtube.com/watch?v=tJq5Dk3PuWk).

3. Paste the URL of the video into your Buzz post. Buzz displays a thumbnail of the video, as you can see in Figure 8.18.

4. Click the **Post** button to post your message.

The video will appear as a thumbnail in your post, as shown in Figure 8.19.

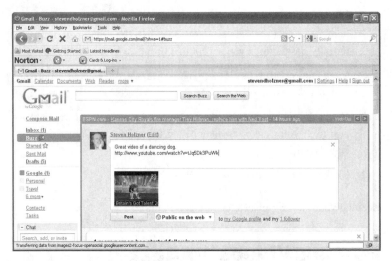

FIGURE 8.18   Posting a YouTube video.

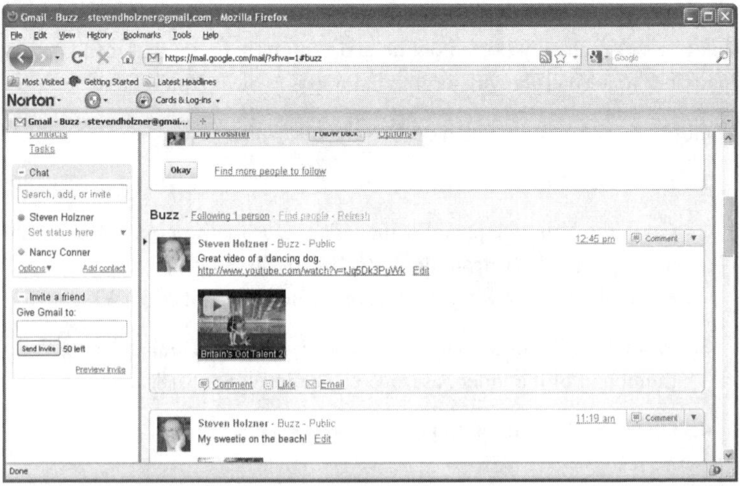

FIGURE 8.19   A YouTube video thumbnail.

When you click the video in the post, it expands to its size on YouTube and plays.

LESSON 9

Using Chat

In this lesson, we'll take a look at one of the powerful features of Gmail called Chat. You can use Chat to type interactively with any Gmail user.

How Chat Enhances the Gmail Experience

When email and Buzz aren't enough, there's Chat. Using Chat, you can communicate in real time with friends anywhere in the world. We're going to see how that works in this lesson.

Displaying a Chat Status

At the lower left in Gmail is your Chat list, as shown in Figure 9.1.

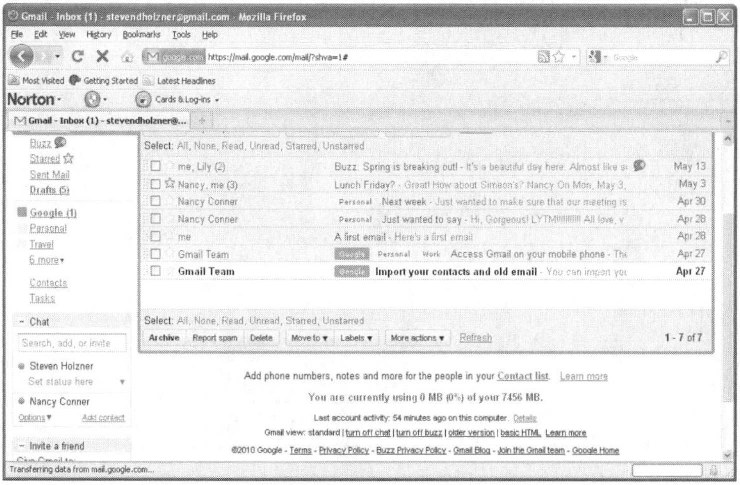

FIGURE 9.1 The Chat list section of the Inbox.

The people in your Chat list come from your most frequently contacted Contacts, and Gmail adds them to your Chat list automatically (you'll see how to manually add contacts to your Chat list in this lesson).

When a red ball displays next to someone's name, that person is unavailable for chatting; when a green ball displays, the person is logged in to Gmail and available for chatting.

> NOTE: **You're Available by Default**
> By default, when you log in to Gmail, your Chat status becomes "available," and a green ball appears next to your name in Chat lists.

You can set a short status text message that will appear in other peoples' Chat windows next to your name. You can, for example, use this message to indicate what you'd like to discuss.

Follow these steps to set your chat status:

1. Find your name under the **Chat** heading at the lower left.

2. Select your chat status from the drop-down list box with the caption **Set Status Here**. This list box appears in Figure 9.2.

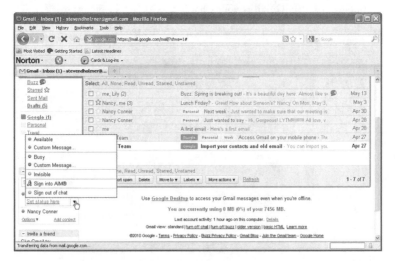

FIGURE 9.2   Setting your chat status.

The available chat status items are the following

▶ Available

▶ Busy

▶ Invisible

▶ Sign into AIM(R)

▶ Sign out of chat

A status of Available means you are ready to accept chat requests; Busy means you don't want to chat at this point; and Invisible means you'll be removed from other people's Chat lists until you change your status.

TIP: **Sign Into AIM from Google Chat**

Here's a tip if you have AOL Instant Messenger—you can sign into AIM (R) from Google Chat. To use AIM (R), you will need AIM(R) buddies that are available to be messaged.

Displaying a Custom Chat Status

You can also set a custom chat status instead of selecting from the available choices that Chat offers you. To do so, follow these steps:

1. Find your name under the Chat heading at the lower left.

2. Select the **Custom Message** item in the drop-down list box with the caption **Set Status Here**:

▶ To set an Available status, select **Custom Message** under the **Available** item.

▶ To set a Busy custom message, select **Custom Message** under the **Busy** item.

3. Enter your custom message in the text box that appears, and press Enter on your keyboard to end the message. The new custom status appears under your name, as in Figure 9.3, where the status is "Let's do lunch!"

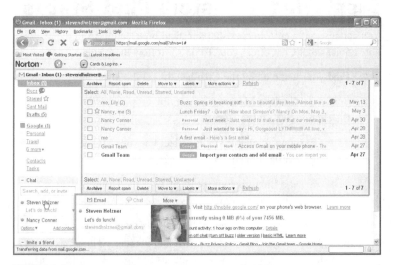

FIGURE 9.3   A custom chat status.

It's also worth noting that your status will appear when people hover the mouse over your name in their Chat lists. You can see what that looks like in Figure 9.4.

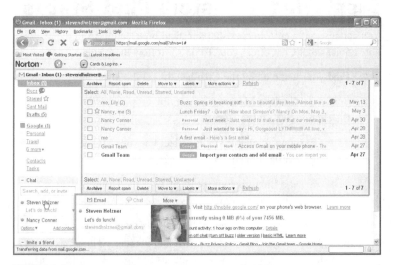

FIGURE 9.4   A custom chat status in a pop-up bubble.

Posting Your Chat Status on Buzz

Want to post your Chat status on Buzz? Surprise! Gmail posts it there automatically.

For example, you can see the Chat status set in the previous task, "Let's do lunch!" in the Buzz stream in Figure 9.5.

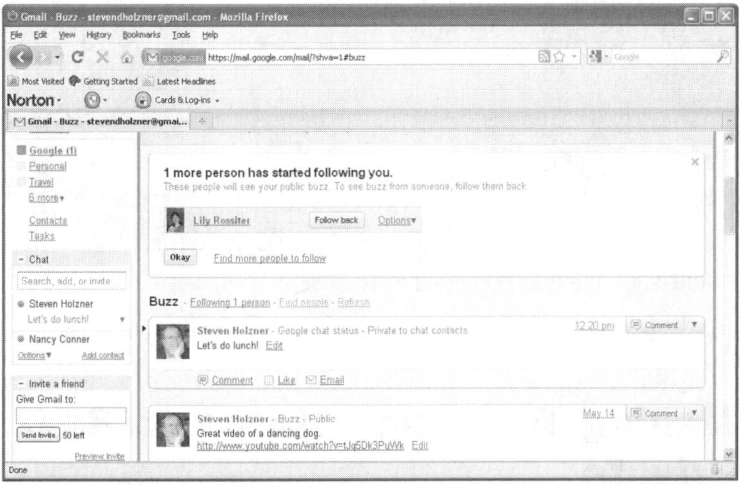

FIGURE 9.5   Posting Chat status in Buzz.

A side effect of posting your status in Buzz is that your followers can comment on your Chat status, if they want to.

In fact, you might not want to have your Chat status automatically posted to Buzz. To connect or disconnect your Chat status from Buzz, follow these steps:

1. Click the **Buzz** link. The Buzz window appears.

2. Click the *n* **Connected Sites** link, where *n* is a number. The Buzz Connected Sites window appears, as shown in Figure 9.6.

3. To automatically have your Chat status posted to Buzz, click the **Add** link next to the Google Chat status item; to disconnect your Chat status from Buzz, click the **Edit** link next to the Google chat status item and click the **Remove Site** link.

4. Click **Save** to finish.

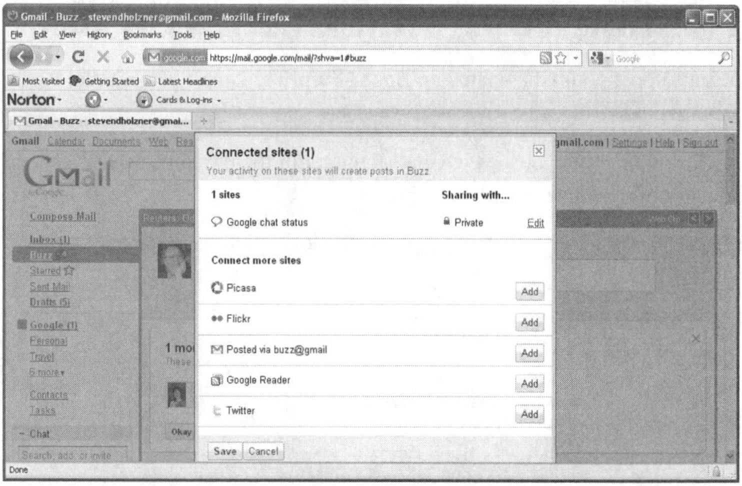

FIGURE 9.6   The Buzz connected sites window.

That's it—now you can control whether your Chat status is posted in Buzz.

Making Your Chat Status on Buzz Private

You can also make your Chat status, as posted to Buzz, private. Follow these steps:

1. Click the **Buzz** link. The Buzz window appears.

2. Click the *n* **Connected Sites** link, where *n* is a number. The Buzz connected sites window appears.

3. Click the **Edit** link next to the Google chat status item, and select **Public** or **Private** from the drop-down list that appears. If you select **Private**, you can also select which groups to make the Google Chat status post private to—click the **Post to Other Groups** link.

4. Click **Save** to finish.

Now you can keep your Chat status private while still posting it to Buzz.

Adding People to Your Chat List

By default, Google Chat adds only your most popular contacts to your Chat list. Want to add someone else, perhaps not even yet a contact, to your Chat list? Follow these steps:

1. Click the **Contacts** link on the left side. Gmail opens the Contacts page.

2. Click the **New Contact** button. This button shows a generic image of a human figure and a plus (+) sign.

3. Enter the new contact's name and any other desired information.

4. Click the **Save** button. The new contact's page appears.

5. In the new contact's page, select **Always** in the **Show in Chat** list drop-down list box. Gmail automatically saves this change—there is no need to click a button.

The new contact appears in your Chat list.

> TIP: **Displaying All Contacts in Your Chat List**
>
> Note that by default, only your most popular contacts appear in the Chat list, but you can change that. If you want to display all contacts in the Chat list, click the **Options** link at the bottom of the chat list, and select the **All Contacts** item.

Getting Approval to Chat with Someone

In Google Chat, you have to get someone's approval to send him or her invitations to chat before you actually send any invitations. So how do you see if someone will accept your invitations? Just follow these steps:

1. In the Chat list, locate the person with whom you want to chat and hover the mouse over the person's name. A bubble appears.

2. Click the **Invite to Chat** link. A dialog box opens.

3. Click the **Send Invites** button.

A message appears above the other person's Chat list reading, "*[your email address]* wants to be able to chat with you. OK?" The person to whom the request was sent will see **Yes** and **No** buttons. If the person confirms your invitation, a green ball will appear next to that person's name in your chat list.

Now that the person is listed with a green ball, he or she is available for chatting.

Approving Someone Else's Chat Invitations

It may happen that someone will invite you to chat, in which case you'll get a message above your Chat list, with Yes and No buttons for a response. If you want to OK future chats with this person, click **Yes**. Otherwise, click **No**.

Starting a Chat

To start a chat session with someone whose name has a green ball next to it in your Chat list, just follow these steps:

1. Hover the mouse hover over the name of the person you want to chat with in your **Chat** list. Note that that person must have a green ball in front of his or her name.

2. In the bubble that opens, click the **Chat** link. A Chat window opens at the right in the browser window, as shown in Figure 9.7.

As you can see, the chat session is already started in the Chat window, with the other person already chatting away. To see how chats actually work, take a look at the next task.

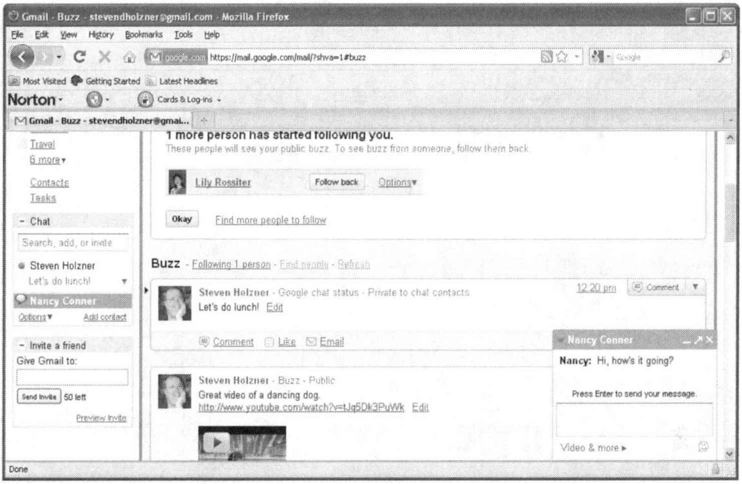

FIGURE 9.7   A Chat window.

Chatting with Someone

After you've opened a Chat window, you can chat. Here's how:

1. Type what you want to say to the other person, as shown in Figure 9.8.

2. Press Enter on your keyboard when you're done typing to send that text to the other person.

3. While the other person types, you'll see a message that he or she is doing so, as shown in Figure 9.9.

4. When the other person has finished typing and presses Enter, the message will appear in your Chat window, as shown in Figure 9.10.

5. Type what you want in response to the other person, and press the Enter key on your keyboard.

And that's all there is to it.

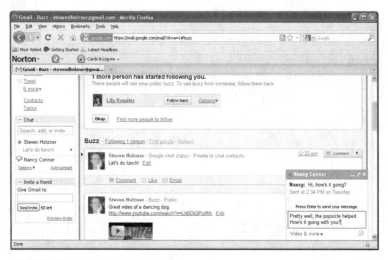

FIGURE 9.8   Entering chat text.

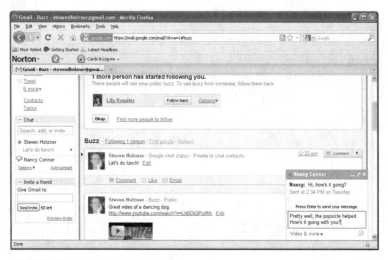

FIGURE 9.9   Waiting for the other person.

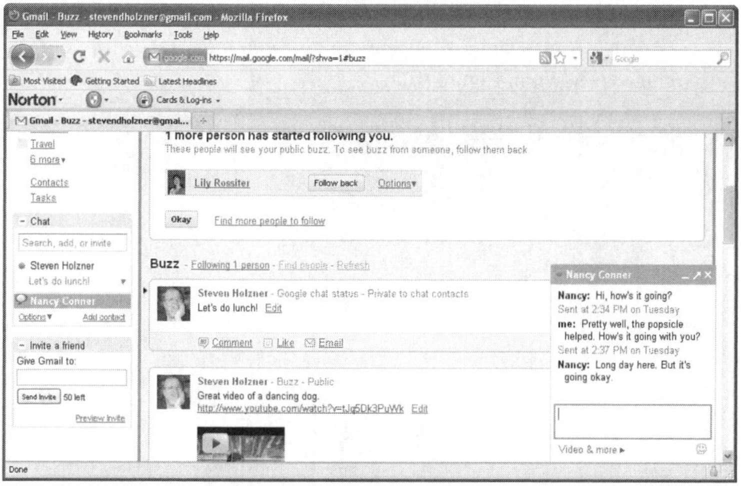

FIGURE 9.10   Response from the other person.

Chatting in Free-standing Windows

The Chat window is small by default and fits into the larger Gmail window. That's fine for short chat sessions but can be something of a pain for longer sessions because you end up squinting and using only a tiny fraction of your screen. Is there a solution? Yes, you can make the Chat window into a free-standing window that you can resize as you like.

To do so, follow these steps:

1. Hover the mouse over the name of the person you want to chat with in your Chat list. Note that a green ball must be displayed in front of that person's name.

2. In the bubble that opens, click the **Chat** link. A Chat window opens at the right in the browser window.

3. Click the button with an upward arrow in the title bar of the Chat window. A new window appears to give you more space for your chat, as shown in Figure 9.11.

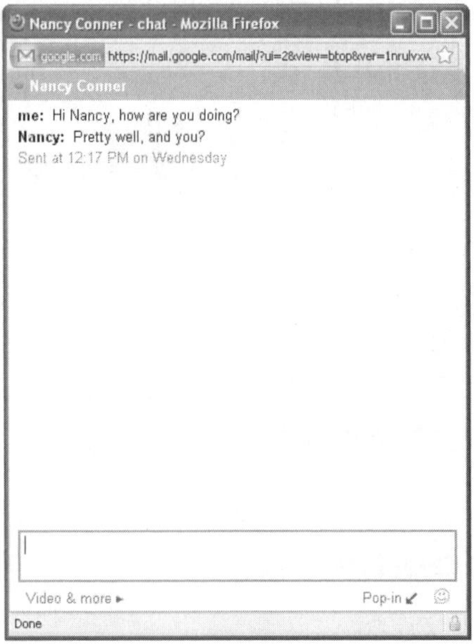

FIGURE 9.11   A pop-out Chat window.

4. Chat as usual in the new window.

TIP: **Returning the Chat Window to Normal**

If you want your Chat window to "pop in" to the browser window again, all you need to do is to click the **Pop In** link at the bottom of the standalone window.

Using Emoticons in Chats

Here's a cute touch—you can use emoticons in your chat. Emoticons are small icons such as smiley faces that emphasize your text, and you can use them to make a point stand out. Want to add emoticons to your chat text? Follow these steps:

1. Click the smiley face button at the bottom right in the Chat window. A pop-up menu appears, as shown in Figure 9.12. Note that this menu is available in both forms of the Chat window—popped in or popped out.

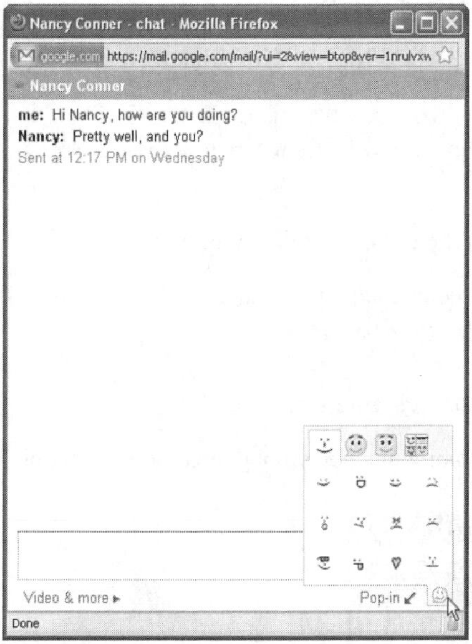

FIGURE 9.12   The emoticon pop-up menu.

2. Click the emoticon you want to add to your text.

3. Continue chatting as usual in the new window. Emoticons can be a fun way to spice up your text.

Ending Chat Sessions

It's simple to end a Chat session—just close the Chat window.

That's all it takes—click the **X** button at the upper right in the Chat window. Doing so removes you from the Chat session.

You might, however, warn the person you're chatting with that you are about to leave. Otherwise, your abrupt exit might be somewhat startling.

Chatting in a Group

Google Chat lets you chat with multiple people at the same time, a very cool feature.

Want to do a group chat? Follow these steps:

1. Within a Chat window, click the **Video & More** link. A drop-down menu appears.

2. Click the **Group Chat** item. A new box appears to let you enter other people.

3. Enter additional people in the group chat invitation window.

4. Click the **Invite** link. All the people you've listed are invited, and if they accept, they're added to the chat.

You can see a group chat going on in Figure 9.13.

Chatting in a group is great for communication among three or more people.

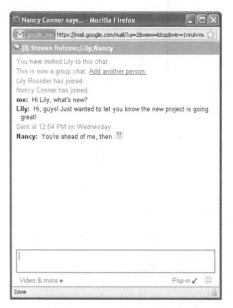

FIGURE 9.13   A group chat.

Blocking People

Sometimes, you might want to block a person from being able to chat with you. To do that, follow these steps:

1. Within a Chat window, click the **Video & More** link. A drop-down menu appears.

2. Click the **Block** *xxxx* item, where *xxxx* is the person's name.

NOTE: **Unblocking a Blocked Person**

When you select the **Block** *xxxx* item, it turns into Unblock *xxxx*. Select the **Unblock** *xxxx* item to unblock the person.

Adding Videos to a Chat Session

You can also add videos to chats—as long as those videos are hosted on YouTube. Adding a YouTube video to a chat session is simple. Follow these steps:

1. In the bubble that opens, click the **Chat** link. A Chat window opens at right in the browser window.

2. Within the Chat window paste a link to a YouTube video into Chat. Chat will display a thumbnail of the video, as you see in Figure 9.14.

3. Clicking the thumbnail starts the video, as you see in Figure 9.15.

Adding videos like this can add a new dimension to your chat sessions.

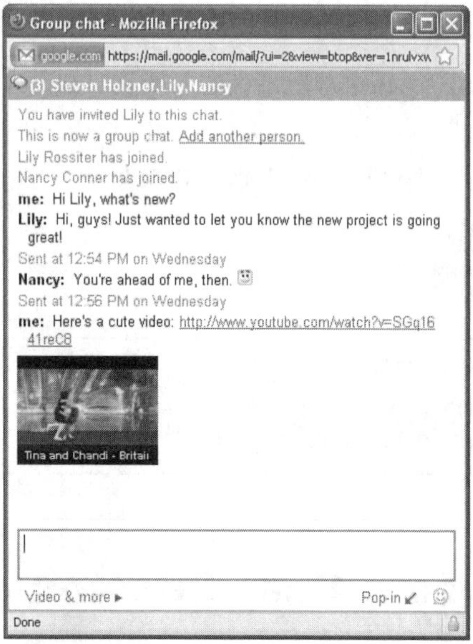

FIGURE 9.14   A YouTube video in Chat.

FIGURE 9.15   Playing a YouTube video in Chat.

Installing Video and Voice Chat

Google Chat now offers an application that lets you chat with voice and video. To install it, you have to download and install some software.

Want to install voice and video chat? Follow these steps:

1. Within a Chat window, click the **Video & More** link. A drop-down menu appears.

2. Click the **Add Video & Voice Chat** link. A dialog box opens, as you see in Figure 9.16.

FIGURE 9.16   Installing video and voice chat.

3. Click the **Get Started** button and follow the directions.

Note that to use voice and video chat, you must have a high-speed Internet connection.

Using Chat History

Google stores your chat history—that is, all the text of your chats. Want to access that history?

Follow these steps:

1. Click the *n* **More** link on the left side, where *n* is a number. A drop-down list of menu items appears.

2. Click the **Chats** link. A box opens showing your recent chats.

3. Click the Chat you're interested in. The record of the chat appears, as shown in Figure 9.17.

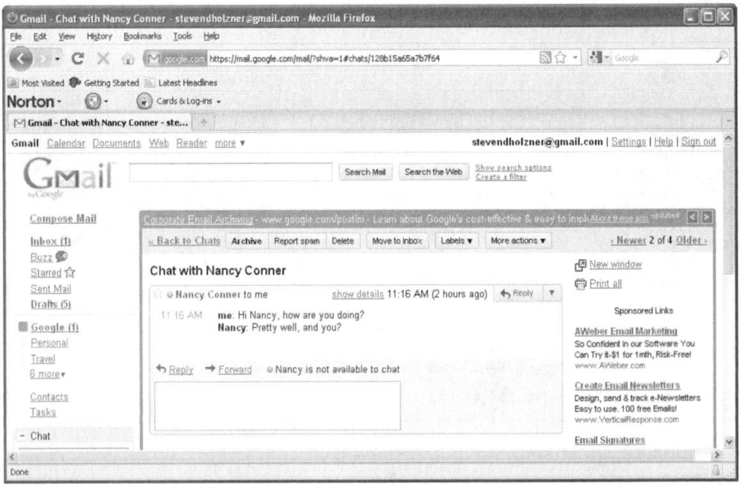

FIGURE 9.17   A chat from a chat history.

Have you ever wondered if you remembered a chat session correctly? Now you can look it up.

Turning Off Chat History

Privacy is a big issue on the Internet, and you might not be thrilled that Google records your chats (a record is kept on your computer, not at Google). To turn off chat recording, just follow these steps:

1. Click the **Settings** link at the top of the page.

2. Click the **Chat** tab.

3. Click the **Never Save Chat History** option button. Chats will no longer be recorded.

4. Click Save Changes.

> NOTE: **Good Reasons for Recording Chats**
>
> Sometimes there are really good reasons to record chats. For instance, if you conduct business via chat, keeping a record of what was said and when could be very important. Also, if your children use Chat, you might want to check in from time to time to make sure nothing untoward is happening while they're online. Like everything, there are pros and cons to keeping a record of your conversations.

You might want to turn off chat recording for just a specific chat session, and you can do that, too. Click the **Video & More** link at the bottom of the Chat window, and select the **Off the Record** item. That chat won't be recorded.

LESSON 10

Advanced Gmail

This lesson takes a look at some advanced Gmail features. Here, you'll learn how to work with Gmail Labs, the set of experimental features that you can add to Gmail with the click of a mouse.

You'll also see how to connect Gmail to other email programs so that you can read your mail from your normal (non-Gmail) program if you prefer, while using Gmail's spam-killing prowess.

And we'll also take a look at some troubleshooting issues in Gmail. If you have a problem with Gmail, take a look at this section—hopefully, you'll find the answer here.

Using Gmail Labs

Gmail Labs contains a bunch of exciting experimental features that aren't quite ready to be made available to all Gmail users. These features can appear or disappear without warning, so the Labs features we take a look at in this lesson may be slightly different from what you see when you go to Gmail yourself.

How do you access Gmail Labs and turn individual features on and off? Just follow these steps:

1. Navigate to the Gmail site and log in if necessary.

2. Click the **Settings** link. The Settings page appears.

3. Click the **Labs** tab. The Gmail Labs page appears, as shown in Figure 10.1.

4. To enable a Labs feature, select the **Enable** option button for that feature.

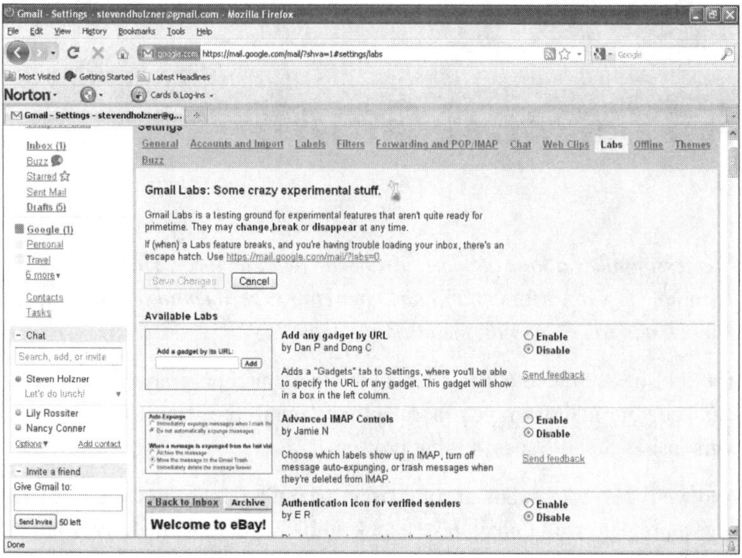

FIGURE 10.1   The Gmail Labs tab.

5. Click the **Save Changes** button. Gmail makes your selected feature active.

This is all very fine and good, but don't forget that Labs is experimental, and things could go wrong. What do you do if a Labs feature jams your Gmail account? Take a look at the next task.

Turning Off Labs in an Emergency

Do you have a problem that you think may be caused by Labs? Perhaps Gmail is not loading properly. There's an emergency escape hatch. You can always access Gmail with this URL:

https://mail.google.com/mail/?labs=0.

And Labs will be turned off. If it was causing your problem, now you should be clear. If not, take a look at some of the troubleshooting tasks later in this lesson.

Adding Google Gadgets

One Gmail Labs feature lets you add Google Gadgets to your Gmail account. Google Gadgets are installable pieces of code that play games, show calendars, and more.

You can find a collection of Google Gadgets at http://www.google.com/ig/directory?synd=open.

You'll need the URL of the gadget to add it to Gmail. To find the URL of a gadget, follow these steps:

1. Navigate to http://www.google.com/ig/directory?synd=open.

2. Click the **Add to Your Webpage** button for the gadget you're interested in.

3. Click the **Get the Code** button.

4. Copy the URL for the gadget, which starts immediately after "url=" and ends with .xml.

To install the gadget in the Gmail Settings page, follow these steps:

1. Open Gmail and click the **Settings** link.

2. Click the **Labs** tab.

3. Find the Add Any Gadget by URL lab feature.

4. Select the **Enable** option button for this lab feature.

5. Click the **Save Changes** button. Gmail adds a new Gadgets tab to the Settings page.

6. Click the **Gadgets** tab.

7. Paste the URL of the gadget into the text box.

8. Click the **Add** button. The new gadget appears, as shown in Figure 10.2.

To disable this Labs feature, click the **Disable** option button for the Lab feature and click the **Save Changes** button.

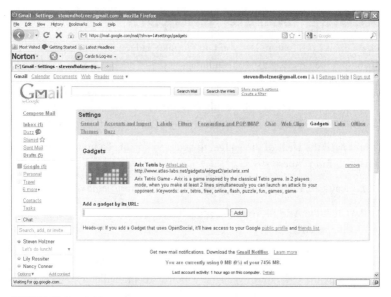

FIGURE 10.2   Adding a gadget.

Authenticating Mail from Known Senders

Certain senders, such as eBay and PayPal, are always being forged by spammers, and you might get phishing mail allegedly from these senders that try to get you to enter account data.

This lab marks every mail message from known senders with a key icon—but the catch is that so far it works only with mail sent from eBay or PayPal. However, it's still better than nothing, Here's how to install this Labs feature:

1. From the **Settings** page click the **Labs** tab.

2. Find the Authentication Icon for Verified Senders lab feature.

3. Select the **Enable** option button for this lab feature.

4. Click the **Save Changes** button. Gmail adds a new Gadgets tab to the Settings page.

That's it—now genuine mail from eBay and PayPal will come marked with a key icon next to the sender's name (eBay or PayPal) in the Inbox.

To disable this Labs feature, click the **Disable** option button for the Lab feature and click the **Save Changes** button.

Using Custom Keyboard Shortcuts

If you're a real whiz at Gmail, you might want to use keyboard shortcuts to speed things up. In that case, this lab feature, which lets you set up custom keyboard shortcuts, should interest you.

> NOTE: **A Few Gotchas**
> Keyboard shortcuts won't work with every keyboard—you need a standard 101/102 key keyboard. In addition, you need to have keyboard shortcuts turned on—click the **Keyboard Shortcuts** option button in the General tab of the Settings page, and then click the **Save Changes** button.

To add keyboard shortcuts, follow these steps:

1. From the **Settings** page, click the **Labs** tab.

2. Find the **Custom Keyboard Shortcuts** lab feature.

3. Select the **Enable** option button for this lab feature.

4. Click the **Save Changes** button.

Gmail adds a new Keyboard Shortcuts to your Settings page, as shown in Figure 10.3.

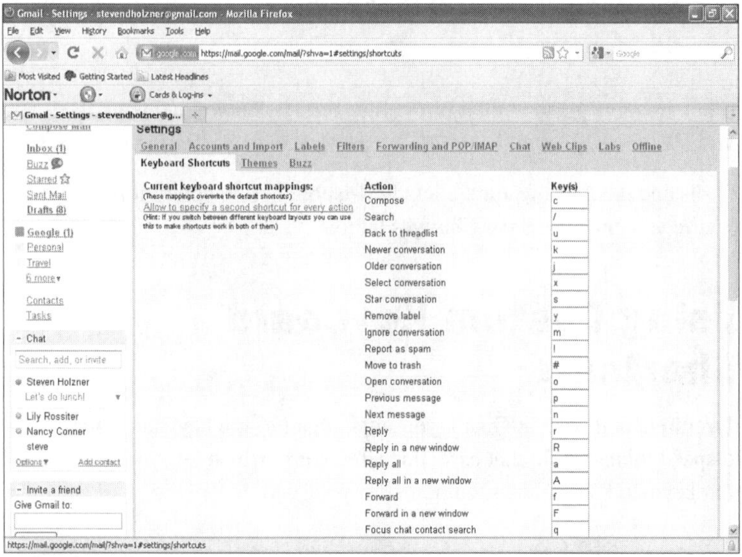

FIGURE 10.3   The Keyboard Shortcuts page.

You're free to reset any keyboard shortcut now—just edit the correct short-cut and click the **Save Changes** button.

Changing the Default Text Styling

You can change the default style of text used in the Mail Composer with this handy Labs feature. Want to always reply with a particular text font? Follow these steps:

1. From the Labs tab, find the **Default Text Styling** lab feature.

2. Select the **Enable** option button for this lab feature.

3. Click the **Save Changes** button. Gmail adds this feature.

That's it—now when you go to the General tab of the Settings page, you'll see a Default text style setting, as shown in Figure 10.4.

FIGURE 10.4   The default text setting.

You can use the small toolbar in the Default text style setting to set the default text style you want the Mail Composer to use. Be sure to click the **Save Changes** button when you're done.

To disable this Labs feature, click the **Disable** option button for the Labs feature and click the **Save Changes** button.

Adding a Google Calendar

You can add a Google Calendar gadget to Gmail to keep track of appointments and meetings. To do so, follow these steps:

1. Click the **Settings** link. The Settings page appears.

2. Click the **Labs** tab.

3. Find the **Google Calendar Gadget** lab feature.

4. Select the **Enable** option button for this lab feature.

5. Click the **Save Changes** button.

That's it—now the Google Calendar gadget will appear in the left column of all your Gmail pages, as shown in Figure 10.5.

To disable this Labs feature, click the **Disable** option button for the Lab feature and click the **Save Changes** button.

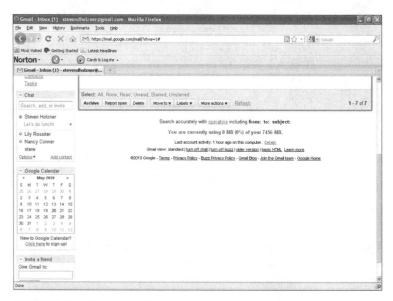

FIGURE 10.5   The Google Calendar gadget.

Coordinating Google Docs

Google also offers Google Docs, an online suite of applications, including a word processor, spreadsheet, and so on, which you can find at www.google.com/docs.

NOTE: **You Already Have a Google Docs Account**

Give Google Docs a try—now that you have a Google account because you're a Gmail user, your Google Docs account has also been set up automatically.

A Labs feature ties a Google Docs gadget to your Gmail account so that it displays your most recent Google Docs, such as spreadsheets, PowerPoint-like presentations, word processing documents, and so on. Clicking an item under the gadget opens the corresponding Google Docs document.

To install this gadget, follow these steps:

1. From the Settings page, click the **Labs** tab.

2. Find the Google Docs Gadget lab feature.

3. Select the **Enable** option button for this lab feature.

4. Click the **Save Changes** button.

Now you can see the list of your most recent Google Docs items, as shown in Figure 10.6 (where I have created a Google Docs document named Favorite Movies as a demonstration).

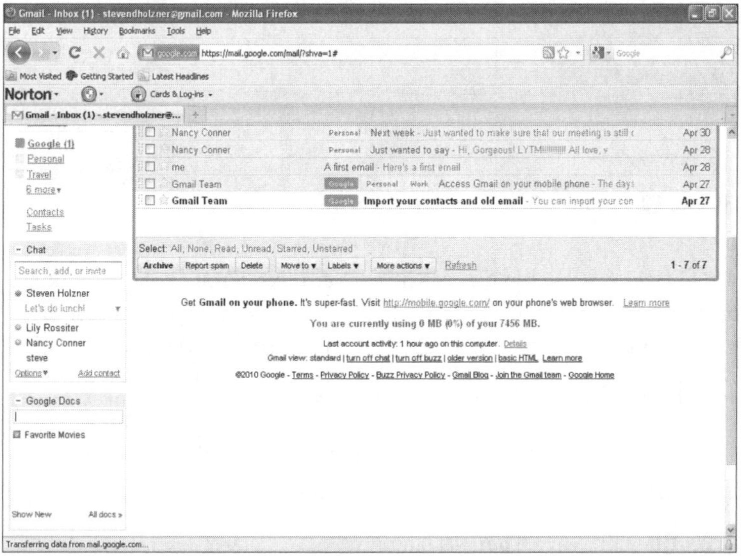

FIGURE 10.6   The Google Docs gadget.

Hiding Inbox Labels

This Labs feature lets you hide labels in your Inbox. You can see some Inbox labels (Person appearing in front of the Subject) in Figure 10.7.

FIGURE 10.7   Inbox labels.

Why would you want to hide labels in your Inbox? You might be working on a laptop with a very small screen, for example, and find it more useful to read a mail message's subject rather than its label.

To hide labels in your Inbox, follow these steps:

1. On the Labs tab find the **Hide Labels from Subjects** lab feature.

2. Select the **Enable** option button for this lab feature.

3. Click the **Save Changes** button.

Now the labels in your Inbox will be hidden, as you see in Figure 10.8.

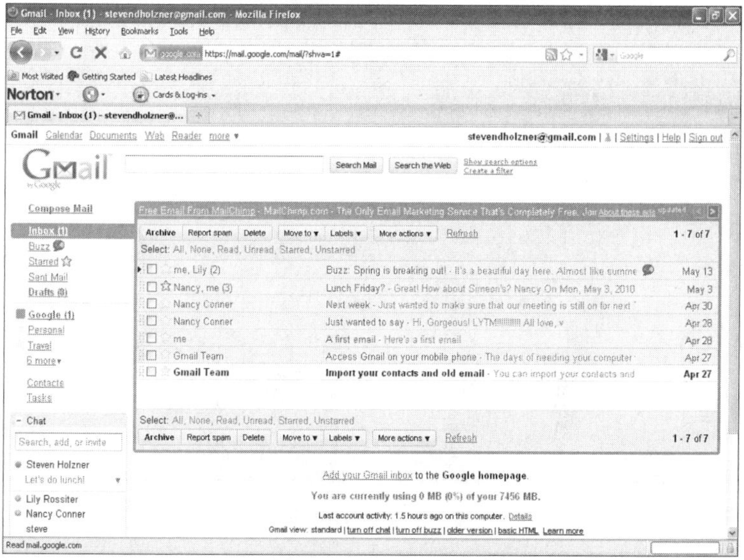

FIGURE 10.8 Hiding Inbox labels.

To disable this Labs feature, click the **Disable** option button for the Lab feature and click the **Save Changes** button.

Forwarding Mail Automatically

Suppose you don't always want to check your Gmail account for mail. If you have a standard email program and want to use that, you can have Gmail forward the mail it gets to another address automatically.

To forward mail, you need to verify that the person connected to the target email address will permit forwarding to that account, so you start forwarding by verifying the target email address as follows

1. Click the **Settings** link. The Settings page appears.

2. Click the **Forwarding and POP/IMAP** tab. You can see this tab in Figure 10.9.

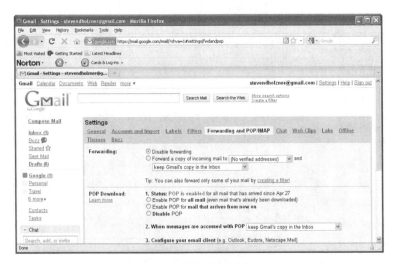

FIGURE 10.9   The Forwarding and POP/IMAP tab.

3. In the Forwarding section, select the **Add New Email Address** item in the drop-down list box. A dialog box opens.

4. Enter the email address you want to forward mail to.

5. Click the **Next** button. Gmail displays a message in the dialog box indicating that it will send a test message to the email address.

6. Click the **OK** button to dismiss the dialog box.

7. In your own email program, open the mail message Gmail sent to you.

8. Click the link in the mail message confirming the request. The email address is now verified.

To forward all your mail to a verified email address, follow these steps:

1. Click the **Forwarding and POP/IMAP** tab.

2. Select the **Forward a Copy of Incoming Mail** option button.

3. Select a verified email address to which you want to forward mail.

4. Select an option for Gmail from the second drop-down list box, specifying that you want Gmail to:

> ▶ Keep a copy of all mail in the Inbox.

> ▶ Mark all mail as read.

> ▶ Archive all mail.

> ▶ Delete all mail.

5. Click the **Save Changes** button.

TIP: **Deleting Unwanted Mail Before It's Forwarded**

If you want to forward only a portion of your mail, consider making a filter that will delete unwanted mail before it gets forwarded.

Using Your Email Program with POP

You might like Gmail's spam-killing capabilities but hate its interface. In that case, you can read your Gmail using your own email program (such as Outlook, Outlook Express, Eudora, and others). There are two supported mail protocols that Gmail can send mail with—POP and IMAP. We'll take a look at POP here and IMAP in the next task.

TIP: **IMAP Over POP**

Although POP works fine when you have Gmail send mail to your email program, consider using IMAP instead of POP if your email program supports it. IMAP allows for two-way communication between your email program and Gmail, so your email program can send back confirmation that it got the mail and make reading your mail more error-free.

Do you want to configure Gmail to send your mail to your email program via POP? Follow these steps:

1. From the **Settings** page, click the **Forwarding and POP/IMAP** tab.

2. Find the POP Download section, and select the correct option
    button:

    ▶ Enable POP for all mail (even mail that's already been
      downloaded)

    ▶ Enable POP for mail that arrives from now on

    ▶ Disable POP

3. In the **When Messages Are Accessed with POP** drop-down list,
    select one of the following items:

    ▶ Keep a copy of all mail in the Inbox

    ▶ Mark all mail as read

    ▶ Archive all mail

    ▶ Delete all mail

4. Click the Save Changes button.

5. To find the configuration instructions for your email program,
    click the **Configuration Instructions** link. Configure your email
    program to read mail from Gmail using the configuration
    instructions.

That's it—now you can read your Gmail with your own email program
through the POP protocol.

Using Your Email Program with IMAP

In the previous task, we took a look at having Gmail send your mail to
your own email program (such as Outlook, Outlook Express, Eudora, and
so on) using the POP protocol. In this task, we'll do the same thing using
the IMAP protocol.

Do you want to configure Gmail to send your mail to your email program via IMAP? Just follow these steps:

1. From the **Settings** page, click the **Forwarding and POP/IMAP** tab.

2. Find the **IMAP Access** section and select the **Enable IMAP** option button.

3. Click the Save Changes button.

4. To find the configuration instructions for your email program, click the **Configuration Instructions** link. Configure your email program to read mail from Gmail using the configuration instructions.

Now you can read your Gmail using IMAP with your own email program.

Troubleshooting Gmail

In the remainder of this lesson, we'll take a look at some common troubleshooting issues.

Plenty of things can go wrong in Gmail, from trouble logging in to opening attachments, and you'll get some help here. One note—if you have any Gmail Labs feature enabled, be sure to turn it off as the first step in troubleshooting. Don't forget that Labs is an experimental part of Gmail, and things can and do go wrong with them.

I Can't Get into My Account

People can't get into their Gmail account for many reasons. Perhaps they've forgotten their password, or they've forgotten their username, or some other reason.

Gmail maintains a page to handle these sorts of issues. If you can't get into your account, take a look at these steps:

1. Navigate to http://mail.google.com/support/bin/ answer.py?hl=en&answer=46346. This page appears in Figure 10.10.

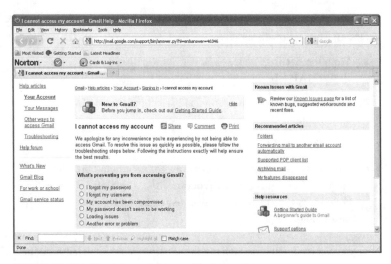

FIGURE 10.10   The I Cannot Access My Account page.

2. Click the appropriate option button:

    ▶ I forgot my password

    ▶ I forgot my username

    ▶ My account has been compromised

    ▶ My password doesn't seem to be working

    ▶ Loading issues

    ▶ Another error or problem

3. Follow the directions that appear.

There are many reasons you might not be able to access your account, and this page can help.

My Messages Are Missing

If some of your email messages are missing, there's usually an easy answer. There are a few things to check first, such as

▶ Check settings applied to incoming mail, such as a filter or forwarding.

▶ Check configuration issues with IMAP or POP access.

▶ Check deliberate or accidental human action or a compromised account.

If the problem is none of these, try searching all Gmail for your messages. Follow these steps:

1. Click the **Show Search Options** link at the top of the page.

2. Fill in the search fields with the details you remember.

3. In the Search drop-down menu, select **Mail & Spam & Trash**.

4. Click the **Search Mail** button.

5. Look for a message in the search results.

Note that sometimes when you're looking for missing messages, they may have been deleted, so be sure to check your Trash.

My Messages Are Not Being Downloaded by POP or IMAP

When you tell Gmail to use POP or IMAP to send your messages to your own email program, issues can occur. The most common of these is that your email program isn't using "recent mode," which fetches the last 30 days of mail, regardless of any other factors.

If you're having problems with POP or IMAP downloading, try these steps:

1. If you're not using recent mode in your email program, make sure that the option to Leave Messages on Server in your POP client settings is not checked.

2. Try turning on recent mode in your email program by replacing username@gmail.com in the Username field of your email program settings with **recent:username@gmail.com**, and be sure to enable **Leave Messages on Server** in your POP client settings.

3. Try deleting your Gmail address in your email program and then adding it again with all the correct settings.

Chat Doesn't Appear in Gmail

There can be times that the Chat list doesn't appear in Gmail, so you can't chat with friends. Here are some things to check to turn Chat back on:

▶ You might be using a browser that doesn't support Chat. Only the fully Gmail-supported browsers support Chat. See Lesson 2, "Signing Up for Gmail," for the complete list of browsers.

▶ You may not be using the standard version of Gmail. Chat is not available in the basic version of Gmail. Scroll to the bottom of the Gmail page, and click **Standard** to select this version.

▶ You may not be using a language that supports Chat. This isn't very likely because Chat now supports 38 languages, but it's possible.

▶ You Chat list may be collapsed. The Chat list can be collapsed so that only a single line appears. If the black triangle at the top of the Chat list points up, click it so that it expands the Chat list and the triangle points down.

Attachments Don't Download

When the mail you get has attachments, but they don't download when you click their link, the most likely problem is security software.

Gmail has an interactive list of security programs that could cause issues with attachments and offers fixes. You can find this list at http://mail.google.com/support/bin/answer.py?hl=en&answer=8822, and it appears in Figure 10.11.

FIGURE 10.11   The security program blocker page.

I Get a Message About My Browser's "Cookie Functionality"

If you get a message about Cookie functionality, it means cookies are turned off in your browser and you need to turn them on to run Gmail.

How you turn cookies on varies by browser; for example, in Internet Explorer 8 (IE8), follow these steps:

1. Open Internet Explorer.

2. Click **Tools**.

3. Select **Internet Options**.

4. Click the **Content** tab at the top of the dialog box. (If the Content Advisor is enabled, disable it.)

5. Click **OK**.

Gmail also advises that you should clear your browser's cache. How you do that also depends on the browser you have; in IE8 for example, you follow these steps:

1. Log out of Gmail.

2. Close all other open Internet Explorer windows.

3. Click **Tools**.

4. Select **Internet Options**.

5. In the **General** tab, in the Browsing History section, click **Delete**.

6. The Delete Browsing History box will appear. Check the box next to **Temporary Internet Files** and the box next to **Cookies**.

7. Click Delete.

8. Click **OK**.

That will fix any problem Gmail has with cookies.

Index

How can we make this index more useful? Email us at indexes@samspublishing.com

Sams**TeachYourself**

from Sams Publishing

Sams **Teach Yourself in 10 Minutes** offers straightforward, practical answers for fast results.

These small books of 250 pages or less offer tips that point out shortcuts and solutions, cautions that help you avoid common pitfalls, and notes that explain additional concepts and provide additional information. By working through the 10-minute lessons, you learn everything you need to know quickly and easily!

When you only have time for the answers, Sams Teach Yourself books are your best solution.

Visit **informit.com/samsteachyourself** for a complete listing of the products available.

FREE Online Edition

Your purchase of *Sams Teach Yourself Gmail in 10 Minutes* includes access to a free online edition for 45 days through the Safari Books Online subscription service. Nearly every Sams book is available online through Safari Books Online, along with more than 5,000 other technical books and videos from publishers such as Addison-Wesley Professional, Cisco Press, Exam Cram, IBM Press, O'Reilly, Prentice Hall, and Que.

SAFARI BOOKS ONLINE allows you to search for a specific answer, cut and paste code, download chapters, and stay current with emerging technologies.

Activate your FREE Online Edition at www.informit.com/safarifree

> **STEP 1:** Enter the coupon code: DVJDKFH.

> **STEP 2:** New Safari users, complete the brief registration form. Safari subscribers, just log in.